The American Bar Association's
LEGAL GUIDE TO
VIDEO GAME
DEVELOPMENT

Edited by
ROSS DANNENBERG

AMERICAN BAR ASSOCIATION
Defending Liberty
Pursuing Justice

Cover design by Daniel Mazanec/ABA Publishing.

Illustrations by Dave Dixon.

The materials contained herein represent the opinions and views of the authors and/or the editors, and should not be construed to be the views or opinions of the law firms or companies with whom such persons are in partnership with, associated with, or employed by, nor of the American Bar Association or the Forum on Entertainment and Sports Law, unless adopted pursuant to the bylaws of the Association.

Nothing contained in this book is to be considered as the rendering of legal advice, either generally or in connection with any specific issue or case. Readers are responsible for obtaining advice from their own lawyers or other professionals. This book and any forms and agreements herein are intended for educational and informational purposes only.

Printed in the United States of America.

15 14 13 12 11 5 4 3 2 1

Library of Congress Cataloging-in-Publication Data

The American Bar Association's legal guide to video game development / edited by Ross A. Dannenberg.—1st ed.
    p. cm.
  Includes index.
  ISBN 978-1-61438-003-0
1. Copyright—Computer programs—United States. 2. Video games—Law and legislation—United States. 3. License agreements—United States.
I. Dannenberg, Ross A. II. American Bar Association. III. Title: Legal guide to video game development.
  KF3024.C6A94 2011
  346.7304'82—dc23

                                    2011025754

Table of Contents

Chapter 6
Web Site Legal Policies *109*

INTRODUCTION

"One of the most important lessons I learned early on was to find a great lawyer."

—Ted Price, CEO, Insomniac Games

» THE CREATIVE SPARK

It's the middle of the night. . . . You're up late coding some mundane project for someone else; or you're sleeping; or you're playing *Halo*® into the wee hours of the night; you're doing anything but trying to think of the next great game idea. Whatever you're doing, it comes to you when you least expect it—that creative spark. It's the moment you will never forget—the idea for the next *Doom*®, *Grand Theft Auto*®, *Guitar Hero*®, or *World of Warcraft*®, the game that will make you millions and will make you an instant celebrity in the video game world. You just thought of a game that no one else has thought of before. It has humor, strategy, puzzles, arcade action, first-person shooter portions, and role-playing aspects, all rolled into one. Your head is about to explode because the ideas are coming at you so fast. You reach for a pen and paper to start writing this stuff down or, more likely, you start typing away on your computer so you can remember all this stuff when you get home from Starbucks® or when you get up in the morning. You type for an hour straight. Having completed your brain dump into your computer, you start to ponder the work ahead as you whisper to yourself, "Where do I even *start*?!?"

This is a common question. Video games have many pieces and components, and you want to be sure to protect all of them as much as possible. You want to maximize the return on your investment once the game is completed and released for public consumption (and critique!). The various pieces of a video game may be protectable under various forms of law in the United States. For example, different portions or pieces of the game may be protectable using patent, copyright, trademark, trade secret, and/or contract law, or a combination of many of them. How do you effectively protect everything? What formalities do you need to follow? How much will it cost? How are you going to pay for all this? Do you need to form a company? Can you just sell your game online? Do you need an End-User License Agreement (EULA)? What considerations do you need to keep in mind if you market your game online or to children? These are undoubtedly some of the many questions flying through your head faster than you can process them. Let's start at the beginning.

Welcome to the American Bar Association's official legal guide for independent and emerging video game developers. This book has been prepared under the auspices of the American Bar Association to provide a resource for developers as they progress through the development cycle—from initial concept to distribution—and it will help developers avoid some of the typical pitfalls that can occur between the moment they get the idea for a new game, through planning and scripting, financing, development, and finally, distribution.

Each chapter contains a general road map for the phase of development covered by that chapter, including the relevant forms and contracts for that particular phase. The contracts come with plenty of background and some selected negotiating tips. This book is *not* intended as a substitute for hiring a lawyer and is not intended as legal or professional advice. However, this book IS intended to make you a better consumer of legal services. The more you know, the better you and your lawyer will get along, the further your legal dollars will stretch, and the happier everyone will be.

» WHO NEEDS TO READ THIS BOOK?

The book is written as though we were talking to an independent developer of a video game. While the prime audience is the principal development team for a video game, anyone involved in video game development will certainly find various aspects of this book useful.

Business owners, software developers, and graphic designers alike will find this book helpful in understanding their contracts, their place in overall game design and development, and how others on the team fit into the picture. Distributors may also benefit from a clear understanding of all the contracts that ought to be in place in order for a game to be ready for distribution.

All too often, books such as this assume that the reader already knows the fundamentals. This book does not assume that. In fact, it assumes you know nothing (no offense). But it's better to make sure that everyone is starting from the same page, that is, page 1. We discuss each step in the game design and development process. If it relates to the legal or business aspect of getting a new video game made, it's in here somewhere.

The mission of this book is to help you negotiate from a position of strength and complete your game with agreements protecting your intellectual property and your investment that will last for years to come.

This book is for you whether you are:

- Beginning a career and want to impress your employer and colleagues with your legal knowledge of video game design;
- Looking just to brush up your skills; or
- A developer, graphic artist, level designer, or producer involved in making a video game or if you work for one of those folks.

» HOW TO USE THIS BOOK

Think of this book as your friend and coach, a resource to turn to when you have a question. Every page contains information that can help you. Work at your own pace but keep going. Even five minutes a day makes a difference.

The business of making a video game goes through distinct phases: 1) initial concept, scripting, and mechanics; 2) financing and business formation; 3) development; and 4) distribution. While most games progress through these phases in this order, sometimes things progress differently depending on the game's design, financing, and complexity, so don't fret too much if you proceed in a slightly different order than that presented in the book.

The Game: *Snowdown*

For purposes of illustration throughout this book, we refer to a fictitious game called *Snowdown*. The game is fictitious insofar as it doesn't exist, at least as far as we are aware. Any similarity to any existing game is purely coincidental and unintended—at least by us!

Snowdown is set on a snow-covered planet whose name is unimportant, inhabited by some hearty settlers who, when not farming in their greenhouses, enjoy having snowball fights. While the planet's climate is not exactly suitable for farming, there are stores of exotic seeds frozen in the tundra, which drew the settlers to the planet in the first place. The central characters, Bella and Bolt, are operatives in the settlers' Sustenance Excavation and Extraction Division (SEED), whose job is, you guessed it, to find new types of seeds for cultivation in the settlers' greenhouses.

Snowdown includes multiple missions, the primary objective of each being to recover a new type of seed rumored to exist on the planet. *Snowdown* may be played by one or two players, playing as either Bella or Bolt, each of whom have unique skills—Bella carries a flamethrower to melt the icepack and soften the tundra, and Bolt carries an electromechanical shovel to dig for seeds. When playing a single-player game, the computer controls the character not chosen by the single player. However, the single player must switch back and forth between Bella and Bolt at certain points in the game in order to complete certain objectives.

Minigames that may be played between missions, or that may be required to be completed before a mission is unlocked, include snowball fights with neighboring groups of settlers, splicing roots together to create new plants, and deciphering riddles to determine locations on the planet where new seeds might be located.

Video Games Are Big Business

```
Make no mistake about it—video games are big business. In
2009, video game sales outpaced the movie industry, bring-
ing in over $10 billion in revenue compared to the movie
industry's $9 billion in U.S. box office receipts. However,
not everyone agrees that video games should be a revenue
stream. That is, there are people out there—especially in
the video game industry—who believe that all software should
be free. It's on the Internet, I can find it on BitTorrent,
or I can just copy my friend's software—so why should I pay
```

for it? OK, fine. You can hold whatever opinion you want.
But let's see if you feel that way after *you* have spent
months on end coding your own game, which you now consider
akin to your own offspring, and someone rips *you* off. This
book assumes, with some exceptions, that you intend to sell
your software for profit, that you are in this to make a
living, or better yet, that you hope to become a video game
millionaire . . . and a video game god.

Copyrights, Patents, and Trademarks

A good idea is the genesis of any game. After you get your idea for the next *Halo®*, *Grand Theft Auto®*, *Guitar Hero®*, or *World of Warcraft®*, what do you do first? Unfortunately, this is the phase where many developers think they don't need a lawyer or a contract—they will just play one more hour of *World of Warcraft*, code the game in their sleep, and make millions. It's not always that easy—in fact, it rarely is that easy.

There are many ways to get a game idea—come up with your own, develop a concept with one or more partners, or perhaps adapt a video game from a book or a movie. Whether you come up with your own idea or want to use someone else's, you may need to acquire some underlying rights, most often adaptation rights of some sort.

It's important to get started on solid footing. Too many folks want to move forward on the creative side of things without taking care of the fundamental agreement between or among everyone involved. They say, "We'll take care of that stuff later," "We're all friends," or worse, "We are all working so well together now, I don't want to upset the apple cart." We've heard it all.

Our experience is loaded with problems that grow out of this attitude. If no one is clear about the roles, the ultimate control of a project, and the ultimate vision for the life of the project, people will almost certainly develop different expectations. When the visions finally clash, hurt feelings turn to anger and then lawsuits—useless, needless lawsuits that would never have happened if folks had taken care of business at the beginning. Remember, just like good fences make good neighbors, good contracts make good business partners.

Business and Finance Issues

Too often, no thought is given to the issues of business and finance until the game's script or storyboard is completed. It is a good idea to have a plan to finance your game even as you work on the initial concept. Portions of this book deal with the basic business decisions you will have to make before you develop your game—whether as a corporation, a limited partnership, or working as an individual. Most folks end up using a single-purpose game development entity in the form of a limited liability company (LLC), for example.

Employment and Development

You need to have a number of agreements in place before anyone writes even one line of code on your behalf. As you hire people to help code your game, you want to make sure that you're not giving away the family jewels to people you've just hired. Many new game designers hire developers as independent contractors, which has pros and cons, so Chapter 4 discusses the types of contracts you will need to ensure that you own your own intellectual property when your game finally sees the light of day.

Distribution and Publishing

This book will discuss various avenues of getting your game published and distributed to the consuming public. The publishing agreement is a key component of getting your game onto user's computers. We will examine various business models that publishers often use, and discuss alternative and self-publication avenues, as well as some miscellaneous issues.

» WHERE TO GO FROM HERE

Look through the book to get an overview of the process of taking a game from an idea in your head to the computer screen. Then find the part or chapter that is of immediate concern to you. That is the best place to begin.

Most people won't start in the area in which they need the most help. They usually choose their favorite area—the area about which they are confident. That's OK. Even your strongest area can get stronger. Then, as you shift your focus to your weaker areas, you'll enjoy the greatest amount of progress.

The most important point to consider right now is that you're already headed toward the winner's circle. The most successful people in life are those who continue to grow. The fact that you have this book in your hand now puts you in that realm. It's not how much you know that counts, but how much you are willing to add after you think you know it all.

Good luck, and godspeed.

CHAPTER 1

COPYRIGHTS, PATENTS, AND TRADEMARKS

Intellectual property is the single most valuable asset of almost every successful company. U.S. intellectual property laws provide the incentives for individuals to take risks, for companies to invest in research and development, and for the Davids of the world to continue to believe that they can (and will) conquer the Goliaths.

Software, including video games, is protectable using at least five forms of intellectual property: copyrights, patents, trademarks, trade secrets, and contracts, each of which is covered below. Different situations often demand different plans for protecting your software, so consider each form of protection below and make an informed decision regarding which form or forms of protection best suit your needs. Chances are you already rely on copyrights, trademarks, trade secrets, and contracts, and possibly patents in more limited situations. As a software developer, you probably already have some familiarity with copyrights, so let's start there.

» COPYRIGHTS

What is a copyright? What does it really protect? Copyrights are perhaps the most common form of intellectual property protection for software, and are often mistakenly regarded as the only form of IP protection for software.

Copyrights date back to old England, before the United States was even born, when the king (or queen) would grant a single person the right to print copies of a particular book in exchange for a payment of royalties to the king. Today, a copyright protects any creative expression fixed in a tangible medium. Copyrights are commonly used to protect artwork, literary works and books (such as this one), music, plays, movies, software, and architecture. A copyright does not, and never will, protect an idea. This is known as the idea/expression dichotomy, and it is a key limitation of copyright protection, so we will be repeating it often—copyright protects only your particular expression of an idea, not the underlying idea itself. Similarly, copyrights do not protect functional aspects of anything. Copyrights are meant to protect *creative* expression, so you will need to protect *functional* creations using other forms of intellectual property (e.g., patents, discussed below). There is often a subtle distinction between function and aesthetics, however, so this is not as simple as it seems.

The requirements for obtaining a copyright are generally easily met. Any creative work fixed in a tangible medium of expression receives federal copyright protection from the moment of fixation. Very little originality is required in order for a work to be copyrightable. A simple smiling face (☺), even if you were the first person ever to draw one, probably is not original enough to receive copyright protection. However, you don't have to venture far before you get copyright protection for your originally modified face, e.g., add a custom mustache, ears, and/or hair of some sort, and the smiling face is now original to you, and deserving of copyright protection.

How does this apply to video games? Well, copyrights can be used to protect the depictions of Bella and Bolt (see the Introduction), but others are free to draw their own versions of male and female operatives. Copyrights protect your source code, but not the functionality performed by your source code. If someone else, without ever viewing the *Snowdown* source code, wrote new software that, when executed, provides the exact same functionality, user interface, and game play as *Snowdown*, that person would not likely infringe the copyright in the *Snowdown* source code, because he or she did not copy that literary expression. Source code is protected insofar as you make original decisions regarding variable names, comments, and program structure. So if someone else writes new source code to achieve the same result, there would be no infringement. However, if that person copied the *Snowdown* graphics and artwork, too, then that person likely infringes the copyright in the *Snowdown* video game as an audiovisual work, because he or she copied the artistic expression of the game's output.

How do you get a copyright? As mentioned above, a copyright protects any creative expression fixed in a tangible medium—automatically! The moment you put pen to paper, paint to canvas, notes on sheet music, type some source code and hit save, or perform any other act that fixes your expression in a tangible medium for more than a transitory moment, you have copyright protection.

Keep in mind that the requirement to obtain a copyright is originality, not novelty. If two people, *independently of each other*, have the *exact* same thought and write the *exact* same source code, or draw the *exact* same picture, they each have a copyright in their work, and they each do not infringe the other's copyright.

Even though you get federal copyright protection automatically, there are advantages to registering your copyright with the United States Copyright Office, and it's very easy to do. If someone else *starts* infringing your copyright *after* you register it, then if you sue that person for infringement, you can recover attorney fees and some special damages (known as statutory damages) that you otherwise would not be able to recover. If your copyright is unregistered when infringement begins, you cannot recover attorney fees spent to enforce your copyright rights, and you can seek only actual damages that you can prove with reasonable particularity.

Copyrights last for a relatively long time. If a copyrighted work is created by an individual, the copyright is valid for the life of the author plus an additional 70 years. You may have heard of copyrights being a "work made for hire" where the employer is considered the original author of the copyright. In such a case, the copyright is valid for 95 years from first publication, or 120 years from creation, whichever is *shorter*. We will discuss works made for hire a little later.

You can download the necessary forms to submit your copyright at http://www.copyright.gov. The U.S. Copyright Office publishes various brochures (referred to as "Circulars") that you can review to answer questions that you may have. Circular 65 is particularly relevant to registering copyrights in computer software. The registration fee, at the time of publication, is no more than $65 per registration, and is only $35 if registered online.

As you may have figured out by now, copyright protection is easy to get, inexpensive to register, and lasts a really long time. So what's the catch? Why not just rely on copyright protection to protect your video game? Simple—copyright protection is relatively narrow when compared to patents, which can also be used to protect computer software.

Copyrights protect only expression—not ideas. Sound familiar? Also, copyrights never protect functional aspects of utilitarian works. If someone pirates your software, your copyrights will likely protect you, and you can sue for copyright infringement because the pirate undoubtedly copied your exact expression, i.e., your audio, artwork, code, the whole package. But what if someone copies the functionality of your game without copying any of the aesthetics? If you work hundreds or thousands of hours creating your game, and someone rips off a key concept or feature of the game without copying the entire game, are copyrights enough to protect you? As with most legal questions, it depends on the specifics. But suffice it to say that if the copied feature is a functional aspect of the game, then copyrights likely will not help you. Imagine that a PC version of *Snowdown* is the first game to incorporate a "mouse-look" feature that allows a user to circle-strafe around an opponent using the mouse and keyboard in concert with one another. If someone else copies that game mechanic, copyright protection will not prevent him or her from doing so, but patents might.

Incredible Technologies (IT) learned this the hard way when Virtual Technologies (VT) copied IT's user interface for *Golden Tee Golf* when VT created *Tiger Woods PGA Tour Golf*. A court ultimately stated that IT's user interface for swinging a club was a functional aspect, and a patent would be needed to protect it. Because VT created the source code from scratch, and also used new artwork and sounds for *PGA Tour Golf*, VT did not infringe IT's copyrights. Lesson learned.

» PATENTS

Patents protect ideas . . . innovations . . . inventions!

Patents provide quite broad protection, but they are more expensive and harder to obtain than copyrights. Patents are granted by the United States Patent and Trademark Office (USPTO) only after a patent examiner determines that the invention is new, useful, and nonobvious. Unlike copyrights, an invention must be new to the world—originality to the inventor is not enough. You must be the first person ever to create your invention in order to obtain a patent for it.

There are two relevant types of patents. A utility patent provides protection for functional inventions such as a new machine, article of manufacture, computer program, or process, whereas a design patent protects new ornamental designs (e.g., the aesthetic appearance of manufactured goods, computer icons, graphical user interfaces, etc.). There is also a third type of patent for plants, but they are not applicable to video games.

All patents must include a description of the invention as well as one or more claims that define the legal metes and bounds of the invention. Determining these bounds accurately is important, because a patent provides a limited but powerful monopoly on what is claimed. That is, a patent allows the owner to prevent others from making, using, selling, or importing an item, or performing a process, defined by the claims of the patent. Those acts would be considered patent infringement. A claim drafted too broadly may be invalid for attempting to encompass what is old or obvious. A claim that is too narrow may be easy to design around, providing ineffective protection against competitors making minor modifications to the invention.

To obtain a U.S. patent, a patent application must be filed with the USPTO, where it is examined by a patent examiner to ensure that the claimed invention is new, useful, and nonobvious. Examination typically involves careful negotiation between the applicant and the examiner. Due to the complex legal requirements of patent applications, most inventors obtain the services of a registered patent attorney.

Once the USPTO issues a patent, the patent owner may negotiate a license with competitors, or sue infringers for an injunction and/or monetary damages.

Because claims are generally drafted to encompass something broader than a specific commercial product, patents can provide broad protection against competitors who might simply try to make minor changes in an effort to avoid the patent.

Say you invented a chair on roller skates and applied for a patent based on this invention. If a competitor then marketed a chair on roller blades, they might still infringe your patent if the claims are drafted broadly enough.

When Should You Apply for a Patent?

In short, you should apply for a patent as soon as possible. Some people think there is no rush to file a patent application because, in the United States, if multiple people invent the same thing around the same time, priority goes to the person who actually invented it first. However, if those two people get into a fight (i.e., lawsuit) regarding who invented first—referred to as an "interference" proceeding in the United States Patent and Trademark Office—they are still going to have to spend hundreds of thousands of dollars trying to prove they invented it first. In addition, sometimes inventors do something that precludes their own ability to apply for a patent. So the sooner you apply for a patent, the better.

The United States patent laws define three primary actions that might have adverse consequences on an inventor's patent rights.[1] Each of the following three items triggers a one-year grace period, sort of like a timer or clock, during which a patent application must be filed in order to preserve rights to the invention. If a patent application is not filed within that one-year window, the invention belongs to the public domain, and the inventor will lose U.S. patent rights, and most foreign patent rights, to an otherwise patentable invention (i.e., one that is new, useful, and nonobvious). For example, if one of the following three actions is performed on January 1, 2011, then a patent application for the invention must be filed by January 1, 2012, in order to preserve rights to the invention.

The "On Sale" Bar

A one-year clock is started when an invention is placed *on sale,* also referred to as an offer for sale, *in the United States*. After one year from an on-sale/offer-for-sale event, an applicant is permanently barred from claiming the invention in a U.S. patent application. An actual sale is *not* required. This is important—the offer for sale need not be accepted! In order for the on-sale bar to apply, the invention, more than one year prior to the date of the patent application, must have been the subject of a commercial offer for sale, and must have been "ready for patenting" at the time of the commercial offer for sale. An invention is ready

---

1. Statutory patent laws are located in Chapter 35 of the United States Code. Section 102 (b) of Chapter 35 states that a person shall be entitled to a patent unless, among other requirements, the invention was patented or described in a printed publication in this or a foreign country or in public use or on sale in this country more than one year prior to the date of the application for patent in the United States.

for patenting when there has been actual reduction to practice of the invention (i.e., a working prototype is made), or when the inventor has prepared drawings or other descriptions of the invention that are sufficiently specific to enable a person of ordinary skill in the art[2] to practice the invention. The invention placed on sale[3] becomes what is referred to as "prior art" that can be used as a basis by the USPTO to reject any subsequent patent application if not filed within the one-year grace period.

For example, if Acme Inc. places an invention having elements A, B, and C on sale on January 1, 2011, but does not file a patent application for the invention having elements A, B, and C by January 1, 2012, then Acme Inc. is barred from obtaining a patent on the invention having elements A, B, and C. However, if Acme Inc. places an invention having elements A, B, and C on sale on January 1, 2011, makes subsequent improvements to the invention, and files a patent application on January 1, 2012, for an invention having elements A, B, C, *and D*, the prior offer for sale of the invention having elements A, B, and C will not automatically bar Acme Inc. from obtaining a patent on the invention having elements A, B, C, *and D*. It is worth noting, however, that the sale of the invention having elements A, B, and C can still be used by the USPTO as a basis for arguing that the combination of elements A, B, C, and D is obvious to one of ordinary skill in the art once he or she knows about elements A, B, and C. Thus, it is safest to always file a patent application prior to making any offer for sale, or at the very least within one year of the first offer for sale of any embodiment of an invention.

Public Use

Any public use[4] of an invention *in the United States* also starts a one-year clock. A public use can include *any* use of the invention, even if secret, by a person other than the inventor who is under no obligation of secrecy to the inventor. A public use by the inventor himself or herself will also constitute a public use. Only a private use by the inventor himself or herself is not a public use as defined by the patent laws.[5] Any public demonstration (e.g., at a trade show), or any public use by someone other than the inventor, not subject to a nondisclosure agreement (NDA) or other obligation of secrecy, is a public use. A public use can also include a secret public use. In fact, very little use and very little publicity

2. A person of ordinary skill in the art is a mythical person created by the courts, and generally refers to a person with a degree of skill that persons engaged in that particular art usually employ, not skill that belongs to only a few persons of extraordinary endowments and capabilities.

3. Offering to sell or license the *patent* or *patent application* does not constitute a sale as defined in the patent laws. That is, the sale must be of an embodiment of the claimed invention in order to apply as prior art that can be used against the patent application. A contrary result might make it difficult for entrepreneurs to raise necessary capital to complete development of an invention.

4. There is a narrow experimental use exception to the public use bar. If a public use was necessary in order to test the invention or confirm that it works for its intended purpose, then the public use bar might not apply. The public use must be incidental to experimentation in order for the experimental use exception to apply. Be aware that actual reduction to practice cannot occur prior to a claim of experimental use.

5. Note that if the public use is performed by the inventor for purposes of gaining a commercial advantage, then the on-sale bar might also apply, depending on the facts of the specific situation.

are required to constitute a public use. A public use requires only that the invention be used in its natural and intended way, even if hidden. This includes, for example, a secret use in a factory not open to the public, where the invention is used to produce publicly available commercial goods. Suppose Acme Inc. demonstrates a computer at a trade show and the computer uses the invention (for example, a computer chip in the computer that increases processing speed). The demonstration may be a public use regardless of what is demonstrated on the computer (arguably even if the demonstration is of an e-mail application or other application that does not use the benefits of the invention), and regardless of whether the audience actually sees or knows about the chip itself.

Even though public uses of inventions are sometimes difficult to prove and easy to conceal, registered patent attorneys and patent agents are bound by ethical obligations to disclose any such relevant activities known to them, or anyone else involved in a patent application, to the USPTO. This duty of disclosure continues until the application issues as a patent. Thus, whenever possible, an inventor should file a patent application before publicly using the invention as discussed above. Otherwise, the inventor should confirm that everyone to whom the invention is demonstrated is subject to a nondisclosure agreement, and at a minimum the inventor should file a patent application within one year of publicly using or demonstrating the invention to anyone not subject to an NDA.

Printed Publications

A printed publication *anywhere in the world* can also start the one-year clock.[6] A printed publication must be tangible, must be a publication, and must contain an enabling description of the invention. That is, the description must be adequate such that it enables a person of ordinary skill in the art to make and/or use the invention. In order for a printed publication to constitute a publication, it must be circulated or be accessible to the public. Printed publications include printed patents, periodicals, journals, books, published theses, newspapers, magazines, and the like. Printed publications can also include white papers, websites, trade catalogs, conference papers, and other printed papers that are distributed or available to the public. If a work is directed toward those of ordinary skill in the relevant art, very little circulation and very little permanency are required in order for the work to constitute a printed publication.

For example, if a conference paper describing the invention is distributed at a conference, and the conference is attended by those of ordinary skill in the art of the general subject matter of the invention, then that conference paper might be considered a printed publication according to U.S. patent laws, and it can be used as prior art against a patent application filed more than one year after the date of the conference paper. Similarly, a single copy of a doctoral thesis located

---

6. Note that, pursuant to another section of the patent laws, if the printed publication is by another (i.e., not the inventor) and predates the inventor's earliest date of conception of his invention (i.e., someone else invented the invention first), then there is no grace period, and the later inventor is barred from obtaining a patent.

in a library of a remote college or university in a faraway country can constitute a printed publication as long as the doctoral thesis is catalogued by the library and is available to the public.

As mentioned above, patent attorneys, patent agents, inventors, and any other persons substantively involved in the patent application process are under a duty to disclose prior art to the patent office, which includes any relevant printed publications. Thus, the safest course of action is to prepare and file a patent application as soon as possible, and in any event before the inventor (or an entity related to the inventor) produces any printed publication regarding the invention. At a minimum, file a patent application within one year of the date of the printed publication in order to preserve patent rights.

Inadvertent Oversights

When an inventor or company receives a patent, it is natural to want to try to exploit the patent by forcing infringers to stop infringing the patent, or to pay the patent owner for a license to use the patent. In the event that enforcement of the patent results in litigation, which occurs more frequently when the invention protected by the patent is commercially successful, various dates and facts pertaining to the invention become extremely important, even to the extent that a case can be won or lost based on the availability of the following information.

Conception

Most countries' patent laws provide patent rights to the first person who files a patent application for an invention, resulting in a "rush to the patent office" when an invention is completed. These countries are referred to as first-to-file countries. However, as briefly mentioned above, the United States patent laws provide patent rights to the first person who actually invents a specific invention. The United States is thus referred to as a first-to-invent country. Obviously, a key date on which patent rights can thus hinge is the date on which the inventor originally conceived of his or her invention, regardless of whether the invention was actually implemented or working at that time.

Based on the potential importance of the date of conception, every inventor should keep accurate records of the date on which an invention is conceived. An example of evidence of conception might be a developer's or engineer's notebook describing the inventive idea, signed and dated by a second individual, preferably someone who has no financial interest in the invention, and also preferably an individual who did not take part in the conception of the invention. Other types of evidence might include e-mails in which an inventor describes the idea to a colleague or friend, a backup tape from a network server on the date that the inventor first created a file or document describing the invention, or initial dates when source code is checked in to a code vault.

Reduction to Practice (RTP)

Just as important as the date of conception is the date of reduction to practice, that is, when a working model or prototype was completed. When two people both argue that they were the first to invent a specific invention, the inventor who was the first to conceive of the invention has rights to the invention, *regardless* of whether the other person was the first to reduce the invention to practice, provided that the first inventor was diligent in working toward his or her subsequent reduction to practice.[7]

Lawsuits can turn on whether an inventor can prove the dates of conception and reduction to practice. Accurate records of these events are often paramount to patent litigation. An inventor can prove reduction to practice in at least two ways. The first is the completion of a working model or prototype. When a working model of the invention is created, the inventor should document such creation, for example, by making an entry in his or her engineer's notebook or printing any computer source code and signing and dating the printout along with having an unrelated and uninterested individual sign and date it. Other evidence may include a copy of the source code checked in to a code vault or other source code management service. Reduction to practice can also be proven by the filing of a patent application, referred to as constructive reduction to practice. When relying on constructive reduction to practice, the date on which the patent application is filed is the date of reduction to practice for purposes of determining invention priority against another inventor claiming rights to the same invention.

Evidence of conception and reduction to practice should be gathered and maintained when the patent application is prepared. Memories fade and documents get lost, so it is often easier to find evidence of conception and reduction to practice when the patent application is prepared, rather than waiting years later for litigation to ensue.

Enabling Disclosure

As discussed above, an enabling disclosure refers to drawings or other descriptions of the invention that are sufficiently specific to enable a person of ordinary skill in the art to make and use the invention. While the creation of an enabling disclosure in and of itself does not trigger any one-year clocks or affect patent rights, an inventor should be aware that, when the invention is completed to such a degree that the inventor can make or prepare an enabling disclosure, the inventor should proceed as soon as possible thereafter to file a patent application for the invention, mindful of the above issues.

---

7. The United States patent laws state "[i]n determining priority of invention . . . there shall be considered not only the respective dates of conception and reduction to practice of the invention, but also the reasonable diligence of one who was first to conceive and last to reduce to practice, from a time prior to conception by the other." 35 U.S.C. § 102 (g).

Provisional Patent Applications

The U.S. patent laws provide for a simplified patent application procedure referred to as a provisional patent application. A provisional patent application is useful because of its lack of formal requirements and its smaller filing fee. This means that a provisional patent application can be filed on very short notice. A provisional patent application, however, is subject to the same legal requirements as a normal (i.e., nonprovisional) patent application. Because provisional patent applications are subject to the same legal requirements as a nonprovisional U.S. patent application, provisional applications should be relied upon only if there is not enough time to prepare a nonprovisional patent application. There are many nuances to determining the propriety of filing a provisional patent application, so this author strongly recommends that an inventor seek the advice of a registered patent attorney prior to filing a provisional patent application.

Foreign Patent Rights

Most foreign countries have an absolute novelty requirement in order to obtain a patent. This means that, unlike in the United States where there is a one-year grace period, *any* public disclosure can bar a patent in most foreign countries. If a patent application is not filed in the foreign country prior to a public disclosure, then patent rights may be lost in that foreign country. The United States is a party to an international treaty known as the Patent Cooperation Treaty (PCT), which allows the filing of a special patent application, referred to as a PCT application, to preserve patent rights in multiple countries simultaneously, without requiring that a separate application be filed in each country in which protection is desired. This special application, however, is a placeholder, and will need to be "perfected" in each country in which protection is ultimately desired by subsequently filing the special application in each individual country within a prescribed time limit, currently 30 to 32 months depending on the facts of the individual case and the country desired. As long as the PCT application is filed within one year of the filing date of the patent application in the United States, the PCT application will be considered to have been filed on the same date as the United States patent application for purposes of determining whether the PCT application is barred by a public disclosure.

Inventors should be aware that any foreign or PCT patent application must be filed within one year of filing the U.S. patent application. Likewise, if the inventor first filed a patent application in a foreign country and is subsequently seeking protection in the United States, then the U.S. patent application must be filed within one year of the foreign patent application in order to claim the benefit of the earlier filing date of the foreign patent application. In addition, if the foreign patent application matures into an issued patent, and the inventor waited more than one year to file a patent application in the United States, the foreign patent can be used as prior art by the USPTO to reject the inventor's U.S. patent application.

If the inventor waits more than one year in either scenario (U.S. first or foreign first), the inventor loses the privilege of using the earlier filed application's filing date for the subsequently filed application. This means than any intervening prior art between the filings of the two applications can be used against the inventor by the USPTO or foreign patent office to reject the patent application.

When a patent owner sues another party for patent infringement, the patent owner will most likely be required to prove the dates of conception and reduction to practice at some point during the litigation. The patent owner also will likely be required to demonstrate the date of first sale or offer for sale, the date on which the first public disclosure was made, and the date of publication of any printed publication describing the invention. The best defense is often a good offense. Accurate and complete documentation of each of these dates is vital to proving the validity and enforceability of a patent. Thus, every inventor should remember the following tips:

- Document dates of conception and reduction to practice, and maintain evidence of these dates in the patent application file.
- Seek patent protection as soon as possible after creating an enabling disclosure.
- File a patent application prior to offering an invention for sale. At a minimum, document the date of the first offer for sale and file a patent application within one year of that date.
- File a patent application prior to disclosing the invention to unrestricted third parties (i.e., anyone outside your company or not under a nondisclosure agreement). At a minimum, document the date of the first such disclosure and file a patent application within one year of that date.
- File a patent application prior to distributing any printed publication describing the invention. At a minimum, document the date of publication of the document and file a patent application within one year of that date.
- Require third parties to sign a nondisclosure agreement before you disclose or demonstrate the invention to them, and before you distribute any documents describing the invention to them.
- *Any* public disclosure can destroy foreign patent rights.
- If seeking foreign patent protection in addition to U.S. patent protection, file a foreign or PCT application within one year of the filing date of your U.S. patent application.
- As an emergency precaution, you can file a provisional patent application on short notice, including the same material that you publicly disclose (remember, however, that filing a provisional application triggers the one-year limit for filing a nonprovisional U.S. patent application and any foreign patent applications).
- An inventor can *license* an invention prior to applying for a patent, e.g., to raise money from capital investors (but be sure to have the potential investors sign an NDA, as noted above, prior to disclosure of the invention to them).

Every scenario pertaining to intellectual property is necessarily fact specific. This book provides only an introduction to and general information regarding intellectual property, and it is not intended to be a complete discussion and does not include a complete discussion of every exception and nuance of the United States patent laws and court decisions regarding these issues.

What's Patentable in a Video Game?

Various aspects of video games are patentable. As discussed above, an invention is any new, useful, and nonobvious process (e.g., game play methods, graphics techniques, user interface communications), machine (e.g., a computer programmed with computer software), article of manufacture (e.g., a disk or storage media on which software is distributed), or composition of matter, and also includes new ornamental designs (e.g., icons, user interface artwork, characters, etc.). The United States Supreme Court has stated that "anything under the Sun made by man" is patentable.

This means that, provided it is new and nonobvious, you can get a utility patent for game play techniques, hardware, software processes, and even aesthetic design (with a design patent). For example, data-processing techniques such as audio encoding, graphics rendering, memory management, communications, and the like are all patent-eligible subject matter if the other requirements (useful, new, and nonobvious) for obtaining a patent are met.

Perhaps some examples will illustrate the point.

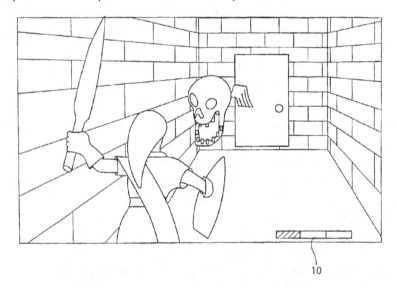

10

United States Patent Number 6,935,954 was granted on August 30, 2005, to Nintendo for an invention titled "Sanity System for Video Game." The '954 patent describes a system where a player-character's in-game sanity level is affected by occurrences in the game such as encountering a game creature or gruesome situation. As the player-character's sanity level decreases, it becomes harder for the game player to control his or her player-character in the game until the player-character's sanity level returns to a more normal level. Representative claim 1 from the '954 patent reads:

> 1. A method of operating a video game including a game character controlled by a player, the method comprising: (a) setting a sanity level of the game character; (b) modifying the sanity level of the game character during game play according to occurrences in the game, wherein a modifying amount of is determined based on a character reaction and an amount of character preparation; and (c) controlling game play according to the sanity level of the game character, game play being controlled at least by varying game effects according to the game character sanity level.

As you can see, the '954 patent describes and claims a particular game play feature.

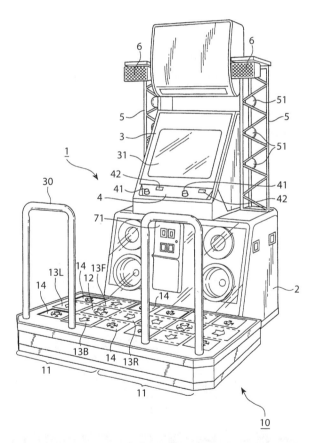

The above figure is from United States Patent No. 6,410,835, issued on June 25, 2002, to Konami Co., Ltd, for "Dance Game Apparatus and Step-On Base for Dance Game" (i.e., *Dance Dance Revolution*). As is somewhat evident, the patent describes and claims the physical arcade game version of *DDR*.

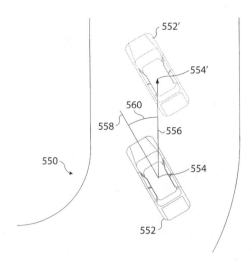

U.S. Patent No 6,604,008 was awarded on August 5, 2003, to Microsoft Corporation for *Scoring Based Upon Goals Achieved and Subjective Elements*. The figure shown above illustrates the concept of the '008 patent, where points are awarded when the player completes a subjective style feat, e.g., driving with style in Microsoft's *Gotham Racing* franchise of games.

From the above example patents (copies of which are on the attached CD), you can see that many different aspects of video games are patentable. When trying to decide whether to patent an aspect of your game, think about what sets your game apart from the rest. How are you going to market your game? What features are you going to highlight? What do you tout to the public and media about your game? These are the aspects that should be considered for possible patent protection.

How Do You Protect Unique Designs or User Interfaces?

Design patents are a useful resource for protecting purely aesthetic aspects of your game. A design patent will not protect the functionality of a user interface, but it will protect the unique appearance of a user interface. For example, Microsoft obtained the following design patent for its "blade" user interface on the Xbox 360®:

 vs.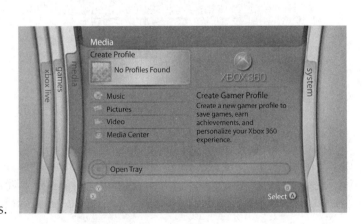

Design patents can also be used to protect unique icons and graphics, as shown below:

Design patents can also be used to protect hardware used to play a game:

As with a utility patent, in order to get a design patent you must demonstrate that your aesthetic design is new and nonobvious when compared to what has been done before.

Patent FAQs

How much will all this cost?

Patents can be expensive, especially utility patents, and are generally regarded as the most expensive form of intellectual property to obtain. First, let's rip the bandage off: obtaining a single patent can cost anywhere from $10,000 to $50,000 to obtain. An "average" case, from start to finish, is typically about $25,000 including attorney fees and hard costs (government fees, etc.).

I think I invented something and I'd like to patent it.
What do I do now?

Talk to a patent attorney. Before you make any public uses or disclosures of your invention, before you offer it for sale to anyone, and before you publish anything describing your invention, talk to a patent attorney, as each of these actions can have a negative impact on the patentability of your invention. If you've already done one of these things, it is even more imperative that you talk to a patent attorney to determine whether you still have rights to your invention, because there is only a one-year grace period in the United States to file your patent application after you've done one of those things.

What will a patent attorney do for me?

A patent attorney will discuss the legal requirements that must be met before the United States Patent and Trademark Office (USPTO) will grant you a patent, and will also discuss your invention with you to learn about the invention so that he or she can draft a patent application and file the patent application on your behalf in the USPTO. A patent attorney may also assist with a "prior art" search, where previous patents and other documents are searched to see if anyone has already created the same or a similar invention as you.

My invention is complicated. Will an attorney be able
to understand it?

In order to practice patent law, patent attorneys must pass a special patent bar exam administered by the USPTO. In order to be eligible to take the patent bar, an attorney must have a scientific, engineering, or computer science degree. In addition to having a technical undergraduate degree, many patent attorneys worked in industry for before going back to law school. For example, Ross Dannenberg was an information systems manager for Carnival Cruise Lines for two and a half years after getting his bachelor's degree in computer science before going back to law school.

Should I do anything to prepare to meet with the patent
attorney? What level of detail and information will
a patent attorney need?

A patent must describe an invention with enough detail so that someone of "ordinary skill in the art," after reading the patent, can make and use the invention. You will therefore need to provide enough detail as if you were describing your invention to a competent person in your own field of work. A patent must also describe the "best mode" contemplated by the inventor of making and using the invention, so make note of any special tricks or modifications that need to be performed or made in order to get the invention to work best. The more of these types of details you can gather ahead of time, the more efficient the patent drafting process will go.

I've seen a patent before, and it had a bunch of drawings. Where do those come from?

Ideally, from you. While your patent attorney may refine the drawings and add additional drawings to help describe and illustrate your invention, you (the inventor) are in the best position to create rough (napkin) sketches or drafts of diagrams, flowcharts, data flow, schematics, etc.

There are a bunch of numbered sentences at the end of a patent. What are those?

The numbered sentences at the end of the patent are the claims. Claims are required to be only one sentence, regardless of length, so they can be a little confusing. However, the claims are the "legalese" that define the boundaries of your invention and specify what it is that others are not allowed to do. So if anyone performs every element of at least one claim in your patent, then that person infringes your patent.

Who writes the claims?

Given their importance in determining infringement of the patent, the claims should be drafted by a patent attorney. Minor variations to claim language can seriously affect the enforceability and scope of the claims, so anyone other than a patent attorney is discouraged from writing his or her own claims so that he or she doesn't inadvertently give up some patent rights. Inventors are encouraged to discuss what they consider necessary and inventive aspects of their invention with their patent attorney, and then the patent attorney will craft and tailor the claims to maximize the scope of protection.

This sounds expensive. How much will preparation of the patent application cost?

Keep in mind that a patent is property and, like any other property, it is an investment. Most attorneys bill by the hour, or some fraction thereof. The amount of time it takes to prepare a patent application naturally depends on the complexity of the invention, the level of detail provided, preparation by the inventor, and the number of claims required to adequately protect the invention, among other factors. Patent applications can cost $5,000 to $20,000 or more in attorney fees to prepare and file, depending on a variety of these factors. An "average" complexity application is usually in the $10,000 range. Additional fees may be charged if a professional draftsman has to prepare drawings from the inventor's or attorney's sketches, typically under $1,000. There are also filing fees when you file the application in the USPTO.

How much does filing cost? The USPTO charges various filing fees based on whether the applicant is considered a small or large business entity, and also based on the number of claims in the application. For a large business entity, filing fees will be about $1,000 plus extra claims fees if the application concludes with more than an allotted number of claims. For a small business entity, filing fees are about $500 plus extra claims fees. A full schedule of fees is maintained by the USPTO at http://www.uspto.gov/main/howtofees.htm.

Sounds like I can save money by doing this myself, right?

You can also save money on a new home by building it yourself. That does not mean it's a good idea. Patent attorneys have very specialized knowledge and skills. However, some inventors do prepare their own patent applications and file them in the USPTO themselves. This is known as representing yourself *pro se*. Keep in mind that patents prosecuted *pro se* are often difficult to enforce against infringers because of various problems, mistakes, or oversights made during prosecution, e.g., drafting the claims too narrowly, drafting the claims so that no single legal entity can infringe them, not describing the invention in enough detail to satisfy the enablement and best mode requirements, and making unnecessary overly limiting statements about your invention, to name a few.

Attorneys recognize that many small businesses and start-ups are on a budget, and will try to work with each client within their financial means, but there is a threshold minimum amount of money it takes to properly prepare a patent application. One way that some inventors can save money is by preparing the first draft of the "Detailed Description" that goes in the patent application. The Detailed Description is where you describe how to make and use your invention with enough detail so that someone of ordinary skill in the art could build the invention without undue experimentation. Think of the Detailed Description as a document that, if you had to hand it off to someone else, would enable that other person to make and use the invention without having to come back to ask you *any* questions. In fact, when preparing the Detailed Description, assume that the person you hand it off to is locked in a room and unable to ask you any questions or get any clarifications. Assuming that person is of ordinary skill in the art, could he or she recreate the invention based on your document? That should put you in the right mindset if you do decide to prepare the document yourself.

How does the USPTO determine whether my invention is patentable?

An invention is patentable if it is new, useful, and nonobvious. A patent examiner will be assigned to your case, and that person will search for "prior art" such as previous patents, publications, white papers, journals, magazines, known products, etc., to determine whether your invention is patentable. The patent examiner will analyze the prior art to determine whether anyone else has already invented the same thing (i.e., your invention is not new), or if your invention is a specifically suggested combination of things that have been done before (i.e., your invention is obvious). The USPTO will provide a written report, referred to as an Office Action, that details its reasoning for why you should or should not receive a patent for your invention.

How long will it take to receive an Office Action?
What happens next?

Application pendency varies, but the USPTO is notoriously backlogged. Expect to wait at least two to three years for the USPTO to send a first Office Action. When you (or your patent attorney) receive an Office Action, your patent attorney will analyze the USPTO arguments, discuss them with you, and then craft written arguments and or claim amendments in response to the Office Action. This is the other major expense associated with obtaining a patent, and it can cost $2,000 to $4,000 or more to respond to complex Office Actions.

The USPTO has determined my invention is patentable ...
now what?

When you receive a Notice of Allowance from the USPTO, you have three months to pay the Publication and Issue Fees (about $1,700 as of this writing). It will then take the USPTO two to four months to assign a patent number to you and publish the patent.

The USPTO has determined my invention is not patentable.
Do I have any other options?

You can always appeal a rejection by the USPTO. The first step is to appeal the examiner's decision within the USPTO to the Board of Patent Appeals and Interferences (BPAI). If the BPAI agrees with the examiner, then you can appeal further to the federal courts of the United States.

» TRADEMARKS

Choose Wisely ...

A trademark is a brand that identifies the goods or services of the trademark owner. Selecting a trademark is an important decision for any new venture. New businesses often try to pick a trademark that describes their product or service, but doing so might result in a mark that is not as distinctive as one that is chosen for its suggestiveness. For example, what if Amazon.com was instead OnlineWarehouse.com? Or what if Monster.com were named ResumeCentral.com? Which is more distinctive and which is easier to remember? Often you will need to spend more money up front when you choose a more distinctive name, but later the dividends will pay off in spades.

All potential trademarks may be placed on a continuum of inherent distinctiveness. As inherent distinctiveness increases, so does the scope of legal protection. From a legal perspective, it is therefore wise to select a trademark with a high degree of inherent distinctiveness. Conversely, some trademarks may possess only noninherent distinctiveness or no distinctiveness at all. At worst, such choices will not qualify for trademark protection. The distinctiveness continuum is roughly divided into five categories, delineated below in order of decreasing inherent distinctiveness.

1. Fanciful marks (made-up words) possess the most inherent distinctiveness and therefore usually afford the most legal protection. "Exxon" for gasoline is an example of a fanciful mark. Because fanciful marks are unique and have no other meaning, their definition cannot be found in an ordinary dictionary. In general, fanciful mark owners possess the greatest right to exclude others from using similar marks on a wide scope of related and less related products.

2. Arbitrary marks possess less inherent distinctiveness because they derive from familiar common words. The word, however, does not indicate what the product is, how it is made, or what it does. "Apple" for computers is an example of an arbitrary mark. Arbitrary marks are still strongly protectable in court from infringement.

3. Suggestive marks possess the least inherent distinctiveness because the word suggests something about the product. Suggestive marks, however, require some imagination and do not directly describe a product or its features. "Nike" (goddess of victory) for shoes is an example of a suggestive mark, implying that if you wear Nike shoes you will be victorious. Suggestive marks are protectable in court from infringement.

4. Descriptive marks initially possess only *noninherent* distinctiveness because they directly describe attributes of a product. To qualify for trademark protection in court, descriptive marks must accumulate "secondary meaning," an acquired distinctiveness based on public association of the mark with the producer. "Forum" for business training seminars is an example of a descriptive mark. After obtaining secondary meaning, however, descriptive marks are protectable in court from infringement.

5. Generic terms are words in the public domain that will never possess inherent distinctiveness. Generic terms are never protectable as trademarks for the goods or services that they define in the traditional linguistic sense, but they may be protectable in one of the categories above. "Safari" for a real-life hunting expedition service is a generic term, but "Safari" for a web browser may be protectable as suggestive.

In practice, there are no clear boundaries between these categories. Rather, marks exist in a continuum, like a rainbow; and the categories are merely helpful terms to describe the relative differences. At one end of the continuum, the law defines marks that are inherently strong and are entitled to protection without regard to secondary meaning. At the other end of the continuum are marks that are highly descriptive and are entitled to protection only to the extent that the owner can establish strong secondary meaning.

Trademark ownership is determined based on who was the first to use the "mark" commercially. A trademark owner may apply for federal trademark registration if the owner has used a trademark or developed a sincere intent to use a trademark in interstate commerce (followed by actual use within a fixed time period). Trademark rights may last indefinitely if the mark is used continuously, although federal registration renewal is required every 10 years.

Federal trademark registration for a mark used in interstate commerce is generally recommended because it allows the owner to sue for infringement in federal court. In addition, the infringer may be liable for additional damages and attorney fees. Federal trademark registration also provides constructive notice of trademark ownership to other potential users.

The test for determining whether one mark may concurrently exist with another mark used earlier in the marketplace is whether a "likelihood of confusion" will result. Likelihood of confusion is increased if the marks are similar in sight, sound, and meaning, or if the marks are used for similar goods or distributed in similar market channels. If a likelihood of confusion exists, then the later mark is generally not available and should not be used.

Trademark rights may be lost as a result of improper usage. A trademark should be used only as a proper adjective, such as BAND-AID® brand adhesive bandages. Words such as "zipper," "escalator," and "yo-yo" are no longer trademarks because the owners of the marks failed to effectively guard against improper use.

Trademark Searches

"It suddenly became clear that not only do we have to come up with a name, we need to do a name search, too."

—*Ted Price, CEO, Insomniac Games*

In choosing a mark, it is important not to choose a mark owned or used by someone else, because this could make you liable for infringement. Prior to instituting an expensive marketing program to promote your new brand, it is usually worthwhile to have a search done to see if any prior uses of the same or confusingly similar marks can be located. An informal, inexpensive search may simply consist of a review of registered marks. A more comprehensive, more expensive search may include reviews of telephone directories issued across the country, marketing brochures, Internet domain names, and directories of trademarks in the United States and in foreign countries where the mark is planned to be used. Whether to use both preliminary and comprehensive searches, or simply one or the other, depends on the level of planning, preparation, and resources that the company devotes to the trademark selection process. The United States Patent and Trademark Office offers a free search interface at www.uspto.gov.

Trademark Applications

To apply for a federal registration, the mark must have been used in interstate or foreign commerce, or there must be an intent to use the mark in interstate commerce within three years. The trademark registration application includes an application form, a drawing of the mark, specimens, and a filing fee.

To prepare the trademark application, the attorney must have the full name, address, and telephone number of the applicant. An application should state the first date that the mark was used anywhere on the goods or in connection with the services, and in what type of commerce, and the first time that the mark was used anywhere on goods or in connection with services in *interstate* commerce. Alternatively, an application can simply state that the applicant has an intent to use the mark in the future. For this type of application, however, you should have an intent to use the mark in commerce and certainly within the next three years. The drawing for a word mark is simply the characters of the mark. At this time, trademark applications can be filed electronically or manually.

A trademark specimen is an actual label, tag, container, in-store display, or part that illustrates the trademark in use. If the actual specimen is very large, a photograph may be adequate. A service mark specimen can be a brochure or other form of advertising used in connection with the sale or promotion of the services.

Applications for registration of a mark are filed with the U.S. Patent and Trademark Office (USPTO). Largely for its own convenience, the USPTO classifies each application according to the subject matter of the goods associated with the mark. At present, the USPTO utilizes a widely adopted, international classification schedule having 45 different classes of goods and services.

Like patent applications, trademark applications are generally examined in the order in which the USPTO receives them. Unlike patent applications, which may take well over a year before the USPTO issues the first action, the USPTO typically responds within six months of the filing of an application for registration of a trademark.

If the USPTO initially rejects the application, the applicant's attorney typically prepares and submits a response, arguing the applicant's position. In the response, the attorney may amend the application and may explain why the description of goods is appropriate or why a prior mark is unlikely to be confused with the applicant's mark.

If the trademark attorney at the USPTO agrees that the mark complies with the requirements for registration, the mark is published in the *Official Gazette*. Absent objections from third parties, the USPTO may then register the mark.

Intent to Use Applications

In the event an entity has a bona fide intent to use a trademark or service mark, it is possible to obtain federal registration approval prior to actual use by filing an "intent-to-use" application. This procedure effectively establishes the applicant's claim to the mark and provides preliminary clearance for registration since the application is subject to opposition proceedings as described below. For example, the owner of an intent-to-use application will have prior rights against another party who begins actual use of the mark after the applicant's filing date of an intent-to-use application. The intent-to-use application procedure can also benefit the applicant because, in advance of investing in the marketing of the mark, it may determine whether any third party will oppose the mark. For domestic applicants, a statement of use must later be filed, with actual specimens, to complete registration.

Expected Costs

As previously noted, it is advisable to obtain a trademark clearance search in advance of adopting a trademark. Prices for trademark searches generally range from a few hundred dollars (for an informal search of registered U.S. marks) to thousands of dollars (for a worldwide comprehensive search). Because of the potential for businesses to obtain common law rights, e.g., in a small local area, there cannot be total assurance that any search has identified every possible relevant third party.

The filing fee for an application covering one class of goods can be found on the USPTO website: www.uspto.gov. If an "intent to use" trademark application has been filed, a statement of use must later be filed with an additional surcharge.

Attorney fees for preparing and filing an application are generally in the range of a few hundred dollars more or less depending upon the complexity of the application. The preparation and filing of amendments to the application varies with the amount of work required to respond to Patent and Trademark Office Actions, and may range from a few hundred dollars to thousands of dollars.

After a mark is registered, there are additional fees when submitting declarations proving that a mark owner is still using a mark at prescribed periods of time in order to maintain the enforceability of the federal trademark registration. Attorney fees typically are in the range of a few hundred dollars depending upon the complexity of the affidavit. Generally, the filing of such documents requires a relatively small amount of an attorney's time, resulting in relatively small attorney charges, as compared to filing a new application or responding to an office action.

You can research trademark registration requirements, and even submit your own trademark registrations, at www.uspto.gov. However, a word of caution—there are many particularities and pitfalls that you may encounter when attempting to register your own trademark. While you may save some money by doing it yourself, the services of a trademark attorney are often well worth it to obtain the broadest trademark protection for the goods and/or services for which you will actually be using the mark.

U.S. Customs Service Recordation and Imports

The U.S. Customs Service can protect registered trademarks from imported goods bearing either "copying or simulating" marks or counterfeit marks. "Copying or simulating" marks are analyzed using a species of the consumer "likelihood of confusion" trademark infringement test. To utilize protection from copying or simulating mark importation, the registered trademark owner must record the mark with the U.S. Customs Service. Among other things, recordation requires a certified copy of the certificate of registration, five copies of the certificate of registration, and a filing fee.

In most cases, the allegedly infringing importer may recover the detained goods by removing the copying or simulating mark at issue by diverting the goods to another nation. The U.S. Customs Service is not required to reveal the identity or location of the alleged copying or simulating mark importer.

Counterfeit marks are unauthorized reproductions of registered trademarks. Under the 1978 revisions to the Tariff Act, goods with counterfeit marks are automatically seized if found. Unlike copying or simulating mark seizures, no customs recordations are necessary to effectuate counterfeit mark seizure. Absent the trademark owner's permission to use the mark, the counterfeit goods will be forfeited and may not be released. The U.S. Customs Service notifies the trademark owner of the seizure and quantities seized. The counterfeit goods are then destroyed. In addition to other penalties, the U.S. Customs Service may, at its discretion, impose fines for entities involved with the sale or distribution of counterfeit goods.

RECOMMENDATIONS FOR PROPER USAGE OF A TRADEMARK

Proper trademark use is vital to preserving trademark rights. "Aspirin" headache tablets and "Escalator" moving stairs are two famous examples of misused trademarks that have suffered "genericide," the public domain acquisition of a once-exclusive trademark. General guidelines for proper trademark use follow.

Identification

Whether used on stationery, promotional pieces, labels, or packaging, trademarks should always be clearly identified as protected by trademark rights. Until trademark registration is given by the USPTO, ™ will identify trademark rights. The ™ may be encircled or used alone, as dictated by artistic judgment. After registration, a small ® will properly identify registered trademark status and rights. Although commonly placed on the right "shoulder" of the trademark, the ™ and ® symbols may be positioned anywhere adjacent to the mark. Through proper notification of trademark rights, the trademark owner can help to prevent "genericide."

In some cases, reason dictates that the ™ and ® symbols not be repeated numerous times for the same trademark in one work. In such instances, the trademark should nonetheless be distinguished from other words, perhaps by capitalizing, bolding, or italicizing the trademark. The use of these techniques is intended to distinguish the mark from the text. Thus, if the surrounding text is all uppercase letters, then use lowercase letters for the mark. In short, be distinctive. Alternatively, a footnote or next comment that clearly identifies the proffered term as a trademark may substitute for ™ and ® connotations.

Play on Words
The parody of a trademark or use of a trademark in a generic manner can weaken or cause abandonment of the mark. Funny or whimsical treatment of a mark, either in editorial or advertising copy, may be used as evidence that the trademark owner does not desire to maintain its mark. Thus, it is important to police your mark and to minimize such misuse of the mark.

Design Consistency
As mentioned above, usage of a trademark must be consistent with the registration for the work; once the mark is registered in a particular form, use it thereafter in that same form. Even changing the word "and" to the symbol "&" in a trademark is considered an alteration. Care should be taken not to combine words, delete hyphens, abbreviate words, use initials only, or change the spelling of words. Trademarks used in ways even slightly inconsistent with the established design can lead to consumer confusion and dilution of the strength of the trademark. This, in turn, defeats the purpose of having a distinctive trademark. Altering a trademark may also lead the public to believe that the original trademark has been abandoned.

Use as an Adjective
Grammatically, trademarks are considered to be proper adjectives. Therefore, in text material, try to use the trademark as a proper adjective—a word that describes or modifies something. Do not use a trademark as a noun or verb. For example, it is correct to state that "ACME products are the best in the world." It is technically improper usage to state: "When you want the best, buy an ACME."

If a trademark is used as a noun, it may lose its ability to help the consumer identify the brand he or she seeks. As mentioned previously, "aspirin," "escalator," "cellophane," and "yo-yo" were all once trademarks, but they have lost their power to identify a source of origin. The public has come to know these terms as the generic names for the products. Band-Aid, Xerox, and Kleenex are current examples of trademarks that are so popular and common that their owners must constantly exercise efforts to enforce proper usage.

Usage by Others

To the extent that others use your trademarks in connection with their products, your marks may no longer identify your company as a single common source of goods. Acquiescence to such improper usage could result in a dilution of the marks' strength or the abandonment of the marks. However, generally others may use your marks in an informational manner, for example, to advertise the sale of products made by you or your company or in proper comparative advertising.

Singular, Plural, and Possessive Forms

Since a trademark should be used in the exact form in which it has been established, a singular trademark should never be used as a plural. It is also a bad practice to use the possessive form, which adds an apostrophe and "s" to the end of a mark.

Frequency of Use

Federal law provides that a trademark may be canceled and the associated rights may be lost if a trademark owner abandons the mark (15 U.S.C. § 1064). State laws are similar. "Abandonment" means that the owner has stopped using the mark and has no specific plan to reinstate use. The nonuse must have continued for a significant period of time. No single specific length of time is established, but it is usually more than a year or two. The critical length of time may vary in relation to all of the facts of the individual situation.

Trademarks are designed to gain commercial advantage, but they should be used properly. Do not let these precautions discourage the use of trademarks or avoid using a company trademark in correspondence or advertising. Trademarks are valuable business assets. They help build public confidence in the product lines of a company. They reflect the goodwill, reputation, and integrity of a company.

» TRADE SECRETS

A trade secret is confidential information that enables one business to exert a competitive advantage over another. Trade secrets often comprise information that is not patentable. Examples of trade secrets include customer lists, manufacturing techniques, chemical mixtures, recipes, and even proprietary software algorithms. If secrecy is maintained, trade secrets have an unlimited lifetime. In addition, they are less expensive to establish than patents.

State law exclusively governs trade secret protection. Under most state statutory and common law, the unauthorized use and disclosure of trade secrets is prohibited. To qualify as a trade secret, the information must actually be "secret" and also must provide a competitive advantage or economic value to the possessor.

Although trade secrets by their nature must constitute secret information, often such information cannot be kept in confidence. This paradox gives rise to permissible means to discover trade secrets. For example, a competitor may purchase a product in the marketplace and "reverse engineer" it to discover protected information. It is illegal, however, to acquire trade secret information by unauthorized access to a trade secret possessor's product or knowledge.

An important business decision is whether to protect an invention with a patent or trade secret. If a patent issues, disclosure of the invention allows competitors to analyze the patentee's efforts, although the invention is protected by law from infringement. Trade secrets, on the other hand, remain undisclosed and confidential. Experience indicates, however, that even when an invention lends itself to secrecy and measures are taken to maintain secrecy, it is difficult to withhold the invention from competitors indefinitely due to proper methods of discovery such as reverse engineering.

After a decision is made to pursue a patent, trade secret protection may nonetheless prove invaluable. Patent applications filed in the United States can retain their confidentiality until the patent issues and therefore bar competitors from discovery and use of the invention.

INFORMATION PROTECTABLE UNDER TRADE SECRET LAW

As previously noted, trade secrets are covered only by state law, not federal law. However, because most states' laws are virtually identical, trade secret protection is fairly uniform across the United States. To date, over 45 states have adopted the Uniform Trade Secret Act. Statutes that are called "Uniform Acts" result from the collaboration of a number of states enacting a statute that is essentially the same in each of the participating states.

Uniform Act

Under the Uniform Act, a trade secret is defined as follows:

> "Information including a formula, pattern, compilation, program, device, method, technique, or process that:
>
> derives independent economic value, actual or potential, from not being generally known, and not readily ascertainable by a proper means, by other persons who can obtain economic value from its disclosure or use, and
>
> is the subject of efforts that are reasonable under the circumstances to maintain its secrecy."

Information that is typically determined by courts to be protectable as a trade secret under the Uniform Act includes confidential scientific and engineering information, designs, information found in pending patent applications, and confidential chemical formulas. Information typically not determined to be protectable under the Uniform Act includes information that is generally known to others in the industry, the identification of customer needs for a product, and the general ability and experience of employees.

The details as to which information can be protected as a trade secret may vary from state to state. The Model Act, for example, does not expressly address customer lists. Nonetheless, some states have modified the definition of a trade secret to specifically provide protection for customer lists. The Illinois version of the Act, for example, specifically includes lists of actual or potential customers and suppliers as protectable trade secrets.

Factors

To determine whether particular information is a trade secret, courts generally consider the following factors:

1. *The extent to which the information is known outside the business.* To the extent the information is widely known, or at least ascertainable, by others outside the business, it becomes likely that a competitor could obtain the information by proper means. Thus, the information is not the type that the courts wish to elevate to a status of a trade secret.

2. *The extent to which the information is known by many employees in the business.* The more personnel who know the information, particularly those personnel who do not use the information to perform their jobs, the less likely it is that the information is truly regarded as trade secret.

3. *The extent of measures taken to guard the secrecy of the information.* If the information was routinely made available to third parties or could be seen by visitors to the plant who are under no obligation to keep the information secret, then courts are less likely to assume that the information is a trade secret and could not have been obtained properly by others.

4. *The value of the information to the business and the competition.* Courts reasonably conclude that valuable business information (such as the chemical recipe for the Coca-Cola soft drink) is more likely to be a trade secret than trivial information that could be duplicated with modest efforts.

5. *The amount of money spent in developing the information.* Again, if the information could have been easily obtained by spending only a nominal sum for research and development, it is less likely courts will invoke trade secret law to protect it.

6. *The difficulty with which others could acquire the information.* The more easily that the information could have been obtained elsewhere or by "reverse engineering," the less likely it is to be a trade secret.

RECOMMENDED PROCEDURES TO PROTECT YOUR TRADE SECRETS

General

To remain a trade secret, the information, which may or may not be patentable, should be kept confidential. Written and graphic data should be marked "CONFIDENTIAL" and restricted to selected personnel. Laboratory prototypes, "breadboards," and production equipment embodying the trade secret should be isolated or concealed during third-party visits.

Limit trade secret disclosures to personnel to whom the disclosure is essential. Also, restrict access to those parts of your facility that regularly have trade secret information. Do not allow individuals who have not signed confidentiality disclosure forms to enter restricted areas. Keep the facility marked as a reminder to those who enter that it is indeed a restricted area.

Ensure that all confidential drawings and other materials are actually marked "CONFIDENTIAL." Of course, such materials should not be sent out to suppliers or sent out for bids to others outside the plant unless the others have first signed and returned an agreement to keep the information confidential.

Courts routinely declare that the efforts taken to protect confidential information must be "reasonable under the circumstances." For example, in the case of *E. I. duPont deNemours & Co. v. Christopher*, duPont had been building a chemical plant. The proprietary process to be used in the plant under construction could be determined by seeing the plant under construction. The process used, however, was considered a trade secret by duPont, and duPont properly prohibited any unauthorized personnel from entering the construction area and viewing the plant. An enterprising competitor, however, hired a pilot to fly overhead and photograph the plant under construction. The Court of Appeals for the Fifth Circuit ruled that the pilot, working for an unnamed agent, had misappropriated duPont's trade secrets. While duPont protected against espionage only from the ground, the court found it would be unreasonable to expect duPont to put a cover over the entire plant during construction to protect from espionage from the air. Thus, the court held that duPont had sufficiently protected the trade secret during construction of the chemical plant and could rely upon the remedies of trade secret law.

Contractual Obligations

Fiduciary relationships (relationships of trust and loyalty) can be established for key employees who must know the secret in order to use it at the company. Such fiduciary relationships should be defined in writing so that a clear understanding exists of their duties and obligations.

To the extent possible, it is generally a good idea to have written contracts with employees, contractors, consultants, licensors/licensees, and assignor/assignees who will develop or who have access to trade secrets or other proprietary information. Make sure that all such personnel know (or have been advised) that they must respect the secrecy of information disclosed to them. Where possible, require personnel to keep the information confidential as a condition for further employment or for further business if the personnel work outside the company. It is a good idea to periodically remind personnel of their obligations with respect to confidential information.

Written contracts do not guarantee that such personnel will keep information confidential. Written contracts are, however, a good first step to ensure that the information will be kept secret. Consult a lawyer to determine the particular agreement for the needs of your company.

Though a written agreement is preferred, the obligation to keep information confidential can be implied without a written contract. The fiduciary obligations of an employee, who knows that certain information is confidential, are frequently found to have been an implicit, albeit unspoken, part of the employment relationship.

ESTABLISHING OWNERSHIP OF TRADE SECRETS

If an employee develops a new device during the course of the employment, a dispute may arise as to who owns rights to the newly developed device. Resolving such matters in advance through a written employment contract can minimize such potential disputes. For example, you can require employees to agree, upon starting with your company, to assign the rights to their ideas, which relate to the business of the company and which are developed during the course of their employment. Again, always consult an attorney when addressing your specific requirements.

Similarly, if there is a possibility of a disagreement with a consultant or a licensee over the future ownership of an invention, then it is best to develop a written understanding sooner, rather than later, as to ownership.

RECOMMENDED PROCEDURES TO PROTECT AGAINST CLAIMS OF TRADE SECRET MISAPPROPRIATION

Severing the Employer-Employee Relationship

After an employee is terminated, he or she should not remove any written company materials from the workplace. Otherwise, the employee may be accused of trade secret theft. An exit interview acknowledging confidentiality obligations is often recommended. In addition, a letter to the employee's new employer commenting upon trade secret confidentiality obligations may be in order.

If a company is considering hiring a competitor's employee, then the company and potential employee should guard themselves against false accusations of trade secret misappropriation. While a company may hire a competitor's employee, the new company should refrain from inducing the employee's disclosure of confidential information from the previous employer. Trade secret information is strictly barred from disclosure; however, the new company may utilize the employee's general training and knowledge. During employee orientation activities, the new company should clearly mandate that prior employers' trade secrets should not be disclosed.

Record Keeping

In business dealings with another company, confidential or proprietary materials may be obtained. The recipient company should have an established written policy regarding how such materials should be handled and protected by the recipient company's employees. Otherwise, trade secret misappropriation or disclosure problems may arise.

Handling Submissions from Outside Inventors

It is important that a company recognize the potential risks associated with outside inventorship. Outside inventors not employed by the company in any way often submit their ideas unsolicited. Courts have concluded that a company may have a fiduciary responsibility to an outside inventor simply by reviewing his or her materials and conferring about the invention. Even when a company independently develops the same invention, such situations are prone to litigation and should be handled with utmost caution.

Many companies simply follow the strict policy of returning all outside inventor submissions unopened. Typically, such returns are conducted by an employee without technical training and without access to the research and development divisions of the company. Consequently, a disgruntled outside inventor will have greater difficulty demonstrating the misappropriation of his or her submitted idea. In addition, keeping accurate and dated notebooks regarding research and development activities will further aid the company's legitimate causes.

≫ CONTRACTS

When you think about intellectual property, contracts are probably not the first thing to come to mind. However, through end-user license agreements, employment agreements, sales contracts, nondisclosure and confidentiality agreements, and various other forms of legal agreements, a developer can ensure that those who have access to his or her intellectual property or video game are limited in what they can do with it. These forms of contracts are covered throughout this book, and thus are not individually discussed in detail in this chapter. However, because knowledge is power, we will go over some basic information regarding contracts in general.

A contract is a legally binding agreement between two or more parties regarding a particular topic or subject matter. Contracts can cover an extremely broad range of things, e.g., sales of goods or services, real estate, employment, legal settlements, and ownership of property (including intellectual property).

Elements of a Contract

In order to be enforceable, a contract must generally contain the following:

- A "Meeting of the Minds" (Mutual Consent): The parties to the contract must have a mutual understanding of what the contract covers. This is generally accomplished by virtue of the fact that both parties to the contract sign the same written document. For example, in a contract for the sale of a "mustang," if the buyer thinks he will obtain a car and the seller believes he is contracting to sell a horse, there is no meeting of the minds and the contract will likely be held unenforceable.

- Offer and Acceptance: The contract process begins with an offer (or more than one offer) to a second party, who accepts the offer. For example, in a contract for the sale of a television, the seller may offer the television to the buyer for $1,000.00. The buyer's acceptance of that offer is a necessary part of creating a binding contract for the sale of the television. If the buyer instead counteroffers to buy the television for $750, this is not an acceptance of the original offer, but is instead a rejection of the original offer and is a new offer that the seller can then accept or reject. If the seller accepts the counteroffer, a contract may be completed. However, if the seller rejects the counteroffer, the buyer will not ordinarily be entitled to enforce the original offer (of $1,000) if the seller decides either to raise the price or to sell the television to somebody else.

- Mutual Consideration (each party must exchange or promise something of value): Each party to a contract must exchange something of value. In the above example, the seller provides a tangible item in the form of a television, and the buyer provides money to purchase the television. If only one party promises to do something (e.g., I promise to give you a gift of $50, and you promise to do nothing), then that is not a legally enforceable contract.

- Performance or Delivery: In order to be enforceable, the action or promises stated in the contract must be completed. For example, if the purchaser of a television pays the $1,000 purchase price, he can enforce the contract to require the delivery of the television. However, unless the contract provides that delivery will occur before payment, the buyer might not be able to enforce the contract if he does not "perform" by paying the $1,000. A breach of contract occurs when one party performs its duties or obligations specified by the contract, but the second party fails to perform its duties or obligations under the contract.

Oral and written contracts are generally enforceable in a court of law. However, various factors may affect the enforceability of a contract:

Good Faith

It is implicit within all contracts that the parties are acting in good faith. For example, if the seller of a "mustang" knows that the buyer thinks he is purchasing a car, but secretly intends to sell the buyer a horse, the seller is not acting in good faith and the contract will not be enforceable.

Public Policy

In order to be enforceable, a contract cannot violate "public policy." For example, if the subject matter of a contract is illegal, you cannot enforce the contract. A contract for the sale of illegal drugs, for example, violates public policy and is not enforceable. Keep in mind that public policy can change. Traditionally, many states refused to honor gambling debts incurred in other jurisdictions on public policy grounds. However, as more and more states have permitted gambling within their own borders, that policy has mostly been abandoned and gambling debts from legal enterprises are now typically enforceable. (A "bookie" might not be able to enforce a debt arising from an illegal gambling enterprise, but a legal casino will now typically be able to enforce its debt.) Similarly, it used to be legal to sell "switchblade kits" through the U.S. mail, but that practice is now illegal. Contracts for the interstate sale of such kits were no longer enforceable following that change in the law.

Oral Contracts

Oral contracts (or verbal contracts), while generally valid, can be difficult to enforce because it is often difficult to prove that an oral contract exists. Absent proof of the terms of the contract, a party may be unable to enforce the contract or may be forced to settle for less than the original bargained-for exchange. Thus, even when there is not an opportunity to draft a formal contract, it is good practice to always make some sort of documentation, signed by both parties, to memorialize the key terms of an agreement, e.g., by following up with the other party to an oral agreement with an e-mail or other message confirming the terms agreed on orally.

At the same time, under most circumstances, if the terms of an oral contract can be proved or are admitted by the other party, an oral contract is every bit as enforceable as one that is in writing. There are exceptions defined by each state's Statute of Fraud law, which states that some contracts must be in writing to be enforceable. Contracts that must be in writing include, e.g., contracts for sale of real estate, contracts that cannot be performed in under one year, and contracts in consideration of marriage (e.g., a prenuptial agreement).

» SUMMARY

The table below summarizes the forms of IP protection, what each protects, duration, requirements, and the test for infringement.

TYPE OF PROTECTION	WORKS PROTECTED	DURATION	TEST OF OBTAINING RIGHT	INFRINGEMENT
Copyright	Authored work (expression of idea).	Individuals: Life of author, plus 70 years; Works for Hire: 95 years.	Creation of original work. Registration is strongly recommended, and is required prior to enforcement.	Copy of original.
Patent	Articles of manufacture, processes, compositions of matter, machines, improvements thereof, and methods of making and using same.	Generally 20 years from the earliest effective filing date (17 years from grant on cases filed before June 8, 1995).	Statutory subject matter; new; useful; nonobvious to person skilled in art. Must file application within one year of publication, use, or on sale date.	Make, use, sell, or offer to sell claimed invention. Export major component of invention. Import invention or product of process invention.
Design Patent	Ornamental aspects of a design.	14 years from grant.	New; nonobvious; ornamental. Must file application within one year of publication, use, or sale date.	Make, use, sell, or offer to sell claimed invention, i.e., same design.
Trademark	Word or symbol indicating origin of goods.	Generally 10 years from issue (20 years from issue if filed before November 16, 1989); renewal every 10 years.	First use of a mark; not likely to be confused with prior marks. Registration is strongly recommended, although not required.	Likelihood of confusion. Dilution
Trade Secret	Information that is valuable because it is not generally known.	Until the information becomes generally known.	Information maintained in confidence.	Misappropriates and uses secret.
Contract	Anything within the scope of the contract.	As specified by the contract.	Bargained-for exchange between contracting parties.	Breach of contract

2

BUSINESS AND FINANCE ISSUES

by Chrissie Scelsi

"Holy crap, we're actually worth something! We better figure out a deal where we are all going to be happy if something goes wrong. . . . Don't assume that, if you have partners, that everything will always be hunky-dory . . . If you wait until you are successful before drafting your partnership agreement, you are in for one giant headache."

—Ted Price, CEO, Insomniac Games

There are many decisions to make when starting a video game company, and perhaps two of the most important are how to set up your business and how to fund it. In this chapter, we'll walk through the various types of business entities, discussing the respective tax and liability considerations, and then examine the different types of funding for a video game company and strategies for seeking them out. We want you to get started on solid footing. Too many folks want to move forward on the creative side of things without taking care of the fundamental business agreements among everyone involved. Don't make that mistake.

» CHOOSING A BUSINESS ENTITY

So you and your buddy have a great idea for a video game, as well as the programming skills to make it happen. A great idea is, well, great, of course, but to really succeed in bringing your idea to fruition, you also need a business model and plan. An important part of a solid business model is choosing the right business entity to protect yourself and your assets. The business entities we will discuss are the sole proprietorship, partnership, corporation, and limited liability company, or LLC.

Depending on the type of business entity you choose, you may need to file a "doing business as," or "d/b/a," with the state in which you are either doing business or incorporating. This can also be called a fictitious name registration, trade name, or assumed name depending on the state. You will need to file for this if you intend to do business under a name other than your own if you are a sole proprietor or partnership, or if a corporation or LLC will be doing business under a name other than its registered name. Registering for d/b/a will allow you to do business under the name of the business rather than under your own name. In most states, the registration of a d/b/a or fictitious name can be done online through the website for the secretary of state.

A critical decision that you must make regardless of what type of business entity you choose is how the ownership of the company will be structured. One component of this decision involves evaluating what each person in the company is bringing to the table, such as intellectual property, funding, industry expertise, and so on. What is the value of each contribution, and how will you reward each person for it? Are you going to give stakes of ownership to the owners of the company? To the employees? As this chapter discusses different business entities, issues of management and ownership will also be addressed. In addition to deciding how ownership will be structured, it is important to also plan for future bumps in the road, by setting up a dispute resolution policy, and deciding in advance how the company will move forward if one of the founders or critical team members leaves unexpectedly. Another important aspect to address is who will own the various types of intellectual property that are not only brought to the table but developed as part of the project, and who will own what in the event the company dissolves or a founder leaves. It is important to address issues like these early on in bylaws or other documents so that if such a problem does arise later, there is a plan in place to guide you.

Another important component of deciding ownership matters is whether the company plans to raise funds in the future, as this may call for a different structure, such as allowing for the addition of venture capitalists to the company's board of directors, the offering of new or additional stock, and/or providing other incentives to prospective investors.

Sole Proprietorship

A sole proprietorship is the legal term for a business run by one person. A sole proprietorship can give you great flexibility in how you conduct business in that you don't have to contend with a board of directors to make decisions and the like, but it does have its drawbacks.

The biggest downside of a sole proprietorship is that it does not provide you with the legal insulation associated with other business entities such as corporations, and if something goes wrong and you end up in court, you can be held personally liable if a judgment is made against you. This can put you, your family, your house, and any assets you own in jeopardy.

Partnership

Another type of business entity is that of a partnership, which typically is formed by two or more persons who are involved in business together as co-owners for profit. Partnerships can take the form of either a general partnership, a limited partnership, or a limited liability partnership. As you will learn, a partnership requires fewer, if any, formalities than a corporation, which can make forming a partnership less expensive than incorporating.

A significant advantage that leads some to choose the partnership structure is the flexibility that this structure provides its owners. In a partnership, the partners are able to choose how profits and losses will be allocated. This can mean that the partners can agree to allocate differently between a partner who contributes capital or property and a partner who contributes services. This can also mean that the partners can choose to allocate profits differently from losses. The flexibility of allocation is not unlimited, however, as some losses are not deductible from income, such as passive losses incurred by limited partners or partners not participating in the business. In addition, the losses such a partner can claim on his or her taxes cannot exceed any gains the partner may have. Partnerships also enjoy pass-through taxation, where the partnership itself is not taxed but the partners are taxed on earnings they receive from the partnership. The partners can also deduct their share of partnership losses from their taxes.

The management aspect of partnerships makes choosing partners and how the partnership will operate very important matters to consider when going into business.

The creation of a partnership forms what is called an agency relationship between the partners, where the actions of one partner on behalf of the partnership can make the other partner or partners responsible for those actions as long as they are within the partnership's scope of business. This is particularly important given that in a general partnership, the partners are subject to unlimited liability for the debts of the partnership. In a limited partnership or limited liability partnership, the limited partners may try to protect themselves by being liable only to the extent of their contribution to the partnership, but unlike a corporation, the partnership does not completely protect them from liability.

The distinction between the different types of partnership relationships available turns on the issue of liability. As previously mentioned, in a general partnership, the general partners are liable for the debts of the partnership. A general partnership is generally not required to file any documents, but having a written partnership agreement defining the roles of the partners and other matters is a good idea. Unlike corporations, which tend to involve more standardized forms, partnership agreements tend to be very specific to the individual partnership, so it can be helpful to consult an attorney for help in drafting a partnership agreement.

In the case of a limited partnership, one partner is typically set out as a general partner who is liable for all debts of the partnership, and the other partner or partners opt to limit that partner's liability to his or her contribution to the partnership. The limited partner also does not actively participate in the management of the partnership and loses some level of control as a partner, but he or she is protected to some degree from personal liability for the partnership's debts. A limited partnership generally must file a certificate, as well as a written partnership agreement, with the state's secretary of state.

Most states also recognize limited liability partnerships, or LLPs, which generally protect individual partners from certain types of liability claims against the partnership. The scope of this protection varies from state to state, and it also varies in terms of the types of claims from which an individual partner is potentially liable, such as tort claims or contractual claims by creditors of the partnership. Some states also require that an LLP register with the secretary of state and provide proof of either liability insurance or assets sufficient to satisfy a claim against the LLP.

While partnerships have their benefits and can be the right entity for some businesses, you need to be aware of their potential drawbacks before choosing a partnership as your business entity. One consideration of choosing a partnership is that while it is relatively easy to add a partner, it is not as easy for a partnership to adjust to a change in ownership. A partnership legally dissolves when a general partner leaves the partnership or dies, which makes it important to include a clause in the partnership agreement addressing the withdrawal or death of a general partner and how a new general partner would be elected. Additionally, keep in mind that the partnership structure might not be ideal for companies seeking foreign investors, as such investors would be subject to taxation in the United States for any profits they would earn through the partnership.

Corporation

A type of business entity that businesspeople commonly choose is that of a corporation. There are more formalities than partnerships with forming a corporation, such as filing with the secretary of state for your respective state, but the corporation can provide legal protection from liability for its owners and directors, as we'll discuss. An important aspect of choosing to form a corporation is the state in which it is incorporated. The laws of the states vary greatly in how they treat corporations, and some are friendlier to businesses than others. A court ruling in 1869 made it possible for foreign corporations, or those operating outside the respective state's borders, to incorporate in that state. This is in part why a staggering number of corporations opt to incorporate in the state of Delaware, including 60 percent of the Fortune 500 companies and 50 percent of the companies listed on the New York Stock Exchange. Now these are typically large companies that opt to incorporate in Delaware, but if you are anticipating eventually becoming a large publicly traded company, incorporating there might be a good idea. The reason the state in which you incorporate matters is that if you run into a lawsuit or other matter in court, a business, particularly a large publicly traded company, would prefer to have judges that are well versed in business and securities law handling their case than those unfamiliar with these areas.

The laws of Delaware are central to its dominance as the state of incorporation for so many companies. There are no minimum capital requirements, and the state requires only that there be one incorporator, which can be a corporation. The state allows a company to keep all of its books and records outside Delaware, as well as having a principal place of business outside Delaware. This means that you can opt to operate your business somewhere outside of the state, such as where you live, and still enjoy the benefits of Delaware's very skilled judicial system should your corporation need it. From a tax perspective, Delaware does not charge corporate income tax on corporations doing business outside the state. It also does not tax shares of stock held by nonresidents, nor does it charge inheritance tax on nonresident holders of stock.

You can also opt to incorporate in the state in which you live. If you plan on being a small business, this can be more convenient from an administrative standpoint, as well as a less expensive proposition, than incorporating in another state.

A potential consideration when deciding which state in which to incorporate is the tax incentives provided to digital media companies that move to that state. For example, at the time of this writing, the state of Florida offers a 20 percent tax credit for digital media projects produced in the state. Canada has a number of incentive programs for video game companies that produce games there, ranging from seed money to tax credits. As the different state and national incentive programs are always changing, doing some investigation as to the current programs that may be available to your company if you are willing to relocate can help offset some of the costs of developing a game.

Another consideration relevant to the incorporation decision is the type of corporation you would like to be: closely held or public. A closely held corporation typically has a few shareholders who own stock in the company but do not take part in buying or selling their shares. These companies often do not pay dividends to their shareholders and have only one type of stock. While somewhat simpler in operation than a publicly held corporation, the closely held corporation faces challenges in the form of personality conflicts that can cause deadlocks in operation among directors. The shareholders of a publicly held corporation, however, usually own their shares as a percentage of a larger overall portfolio, and they are interested in the share price rather than the performance of the company. These shareholders, unlike those in a closely held corporation who may fight in the event they are dissatisfied with company performance, will typically sell their shares when dissatisfied rather than fight to change how the company is run.

The incorporation process is largely the same from state to state, and you can check the relevant laws of the respective state you choose for the requirements and fees associated with incorporating. The first step in the process is to visit the website of the secretary of state for the state in which you wish to incorporate to check the specific requirements, forms, and fees. Most states offer the ability to file incorporation documents for corporations and other business entities online. However, it is a good idea to print out the forms and review the information you will be asked to provide so you can gather that information and prepare other relevant documents. The first step in the incorporation process is to file the articles of incorporation, which typically include:

- The proposed name of the corporation
- The address of the principal office
- The purpose for which the corporation is organized
- The number of shares of stock that will be issued
- The class or classes of stock that will be issued
- The value of the stock that will be issued
- The initial officers and/or directors
- The name and address of the registered agent
- The name and address of the incorporator
- Indemnification, or how the corporation will protect officers, directors, employees, and agents against liabilities they may incur as a result of their activities on behalf of the corporation

In addition, depending on the state in which you incorporate, there may be restrictions on how a corporation may vote and what rights owners of certain classes of stock may possess. It is best to consult an attorney to assist you in the drafting of your articles of incorporation and bylaws to ensure you are in compliance with state and federal laws, particularly as they apply to issuing stock. Issues that can vary from state to state in terms of stock ownership and voting include:

- *Cumulative voting.* This type of voting gives shareholders a number of votes determined by multiplying their number of shares held by the number of directors to be elected and allows the shareholders to distribute their votes among the directors as they see fit.
- *Supermajority.* This means that it would take more than a simple majority to vote for certain actions by shareholders or directors. Stating a threshold percentage is a good idea.

- *Preemptive rights.* This means that an investor would be able to purchase enough shares of future financing rounds to keep his or her current percentage of ownership.
- *Consideration.* Depending on the state, the law may limit what types of payment can be used to purchase stock.

Once the incorporation process is complete, certain formalities must be addressed. First, the corporate bylaws must be drafted. Second, you will need to have an organizational meeting. A corporation typically is governed by a board of directors, and if you are opting for this structure, you will need to name the directors at this meeting, as well as adopt bylaws and appoint officers for the corporation. If stock is to be issued in the company, it will need to be issued at this first meeting as well. An important consideration when it comes to issuing stock to owners or founders or key employees is when that stock will vest, or become owned by that person. A good rule of thumb is to include a "shelf" in your stock-vesting clauses, typically after one year of service to the company. Keeping ownership of a company under control can be important as a company grows and generates interest. Recent news stories have detailed how Facebook and Zynga have put hefty fees in place for employees selling or moving shares of their respective stocks, which is speculated to be motivated in part by a concern about preventing large concentrations of outside ownership of shares.

As corporations can issue different classes of stock to owners, investors, and board members, it is important to address the following in your corporate bylaws:

- Where the corporation will be located
- Setting up how, when, and where stockholders' meetings will be held
- The procedure for how stock certificates will be issued, paid, and transferred
- The number of directors the corporation will have, how they will be elected, what powers they will have, as well as when and how they will meet
- The officers that the board will have, how these officers will be chosen or elected, and what powers these officers will have
- Dispute resolution

Another important provision to include in your bylaws/articles is how disputes between owners or board members will be handled. Many businesses are now opting to pursue what is called alternative dispute resolution as a means of resolving disputes rather than through litigation, which can be lengthy and expensive. Alternative dispute resolution typically refers to mediation or arbitration, which can be binding or nonbinding. Mediation refers to a process where the disputing parties will meet with a neutral third party who attempts to settle the dispute by acting as a go-between for the two parties. It can be done prior to the filing of a lawsuit, at the option of the parties, or can be ordered by the court after a lawsuit has been filed. In mediation, parties can often air differences in a confidential setting that they might not want to air publicly in court. While the mediator works to facilitate reaching a settlement between the parties, he or she does not make a ruling on the dispute—that is up to the parties.

Another form of alternative dispute resolution is arbitration. Unlike a mediation, in an arbitration, either the arbitrator or a panel of arbitrators will make a ruling on the dispute. This ruling can be binding, in which case the decision of the arbitrator is final, or nonbinding, in which case if one party is dissatisfied with the arbitrator's ruling he or she can proceed with a lawsuit in court.

In addition to deciding on a type of dispute resolution mechanism, it is important to consider when such dispute resolution would be sought if one did arise in your company. The location, or venue, where the dispute resolution will be held is also an issue for you to consider. Typically, for the sake of convenience, you would want the location to be in the county in which you operate your business. The same is true for choosing the courts where a disputing party is to file suit in the event a dispute reaches that level. While you cannot always control this provision in contracts between your company and other companies, you can try to do so for disputes within your company.

Removal/Exit

Another important set of clauses to include in your bylaws/articles is a procedure for dealing with the exit of a founder or owner, as well as under what circumstances an owner or member of the board of directors may be removed. This will involve deciding whether an owner or director can be removed for cause or without cause, and what the definition of "for cause" will be. This can depend on whether your state is a right-to-work state, as well as other laws. In addition, you will want to address whether the company can buy back stock from an owner, director, or founder should the person choose to leave the company, and the effect that would have on his or her stock in the company vesting in the future. An important matter to consider when planning for the potential departure of employees or founders is trying to keep them from going to work for a competitor and sharing confidential information right after leaving your company. In order to protect your company against such problems, it is best to include a nondisclosure agreement, as well as noncompete and nonsolicitation clauses in your employment agreement. A noncompete clause will spell out how long a former employee is restricted from going to work for a competitor, and even within what geographic area he or she is restricted from working in relation to your company. A nonsolicitation clause will further restrict former employees from trying to recruit your employees away to another company for a specified period of time. An example of a nondisclosure agreement can be found in Chapter 4 for your consideration.

Consulting an attorney to help you with drafting such provisions can be helpful; however, if you opt to do it yourself, it is generally a good idea to avoid including as reasons anything that would violate employment laws—race, gender, disability, and the like. In particular, the drafting of a noncompete clause will depend largely on state law, and an attorney can guide you as to your state's respective laws about how long you can prevent a former employee from joining a competitor, what geographic limitations you can place on that person, and other matters.

Sample Noncompete Clause

After expiration or termination of this agreement, Employee agrees not to set up in business as a direct competitor of Company within a radius of [number of] miles of [Company Name and Location] for a period of [Measure of Time, i.e., months or years] following the expiration or termination of this agreement.

Sample Nonsolicitation Clause

During the period of Employee's employment and for a period of [time period] after termination of Employee's employment at Company for any reason, Employee shall not, on his or her own behalf or on behalf of any person, firm, or corporation, or in any capacity whatsoever, (i) solicit any persons or entities with which Company had contracts or was negotiating contracts relating to any of Company's products or services during the term of Employee's employment, or (ii) induce, suggest, persuade, or recommend to any such persons or entities that they terminate, alter, or refrain from renewing their relationship with Company or become a client or licensee of Employee or any third party, or (iii) recruit for employment or hire any individual who at the time is, or within [time period] prior thereto was, employed by Company as an employee, consultant, or other independent agent; and Employee shall not induce or permit any other person to approach any such person or entity for any such purpose.

Once incorporated, the corporation must file an annual report each year with the secretary of state in the state of incorporation. Failure to file this report in a timely fashion can result in the corporation being what is called administratively dissolved. This means that the state declares the corporation to have been dissolved for failure to comply with the annual report requirement, and the protection of the entity is lost in the process. In addition, the corporation must file to be reinstated and pay an additional fee to regain its active status with the state. To avoid headaches in this area, put a reminder in your calendar well ahead of the due date for the annual report and be sure to submit it on time. This will also help to continuously keep in place the liability protection a corporation can provide its owners. The last thing you want to find out in the event of a lawsuit is that your corporation was dissolved administratively and that you are now potentially personally liable for a judgment and your assets are now at risk because someone neglected to file the form. An attorney or accountant can help you set up a system to remind you of when it is time to file annual reports and other documents to avoid such problems.

C-Corporation

Another consideration in forming a corporation is whether to treat it as what is called a "C-corp" or an "S-corp." This is a tax issue, so consulting with a CPA is probably a good idea in making this decision. For a "C-corp," the taxation is different than it is for a partnership or other types of business entities, and results in double taxation. The corporation is taxed on its profits, and then its shareholders are taxed individually on distributions they receive from the corporation. Additionally, shareholders of a C-corporation are not permitted to deduct losses of the corporation on their tax returns.

S-Corporation

By comparison, for an "S-corp" the profits of the corporation are not subject to double taxation, and the losses flow through to the shareholders. The shareholders can then report their income or losses from the corporation on their personal income tax returns and pay at their respective tax rate. The S-corporation is subject to more restrictions as to its stock and who may own shares. In order to qualify to elect this status, the corporation must:

- Be a domestic corporation
- Have only shareholders that include individuals, certain trusts, and estates, and may not include partnerships, corporations, or nonresident aliens as shareholders
- Have no more than 100 shareholders
- Have one class of stock
- Not be an ineligible corporation

In order to elect for S-corporation status, the corporation must submit Form 2553 to the Internal Revenue Service with the signatures of all shareholders required to consent to the election.

While a significant advantage of the corporation entity is that incorporation creates a separate legal personality from its owners, it is not a license to go wild with your business practices. In the event of a lawsuit, the courts can do what is called "pierce the corporate veil" and find liability on the part of the corporation's owners rather than the corporation. This is typically found in situations where an owner is found to have used the corporation as an alter ego such that the owner violated the bylaws of the corporation and resulted in harm to it, for example, using the company account as a personal slush fund until the corporation could not pay its bills. So, it goes almost without saying that in all your business practices you should be diligent in adhering to the bylaws and practices set forth in them.

Limited Liability Company

The newest business entity on the scene is that of the limited liability company, or LLC. Developed in Wyoming in 1977, the LLC is a partnership/corporation hybrid that provides some of the benefits of both while avoiding some of the drawbacks. LLCs enjoy the tax advantages of partnerships but still provide the liability protection aspects of a corporation to its board of directors. While there is greater flexibility in terms of management for this type of business entity, there are certain types of businesses that cannot be LLCs. This typically applies to banks and insurance companies, but it is a good idea to check and make sure that your business is permitted to take this form. An LLC also is not subject to some of the restrictions placed on S-corps, such as the number and type of shareholders. Unlike a corporation, the owners of an LLC are referred to as members. The members of an LLC are not limited to certain categories, and can include individuals, corporations, other LLCs, or entities outside the United States. An LLC may also be formed by one owner, and it is then referred to as a "single-member" LLC. This is meant to be an overview of how LLCs are treated; it is best to also check as to what the requirements are in your state.

Much as the LLC provides a great deal of management flexibility, it also provides owners with flexibility as to how the LLC will be taxed. An owner of a single-member LLC can elect to be taxed either as a corporation, a partnership, or as a "disregarded entity." The owner of the single-member LLC must elect to the IRS as to which status the LLC will be taxed, and if the owner does not elect, he or she will be taxed as a sole proprietorship. There have been changes to the laws in some states in regard to how single-member LLCs are treated for purposes of employment and other taxes. It is best to consult with your accountant on these matters to see how these changes may affect your business. An LLC with two or more members can elect to have the LLC taxed as either a partnership or a corporation.

The management flexibility that can be found in an LLC stems from the fact that LLCs can be either member-managed or manager-managed. In a member-managed LLC, all of the members of the LLC control how the business is governed, including matters of how profits and losses are shared and election of directors, among others. Like in a corporation, the members who manage the LLC are subject to a duty of loyalty and care to the LLC, and are expected to conduct business in a way that does not intentionally harm it. LLCs can also be manager-managed, where the members opt to select a manager to run the business. In this situation, only the manager has a duty of care and loyalty to the LLC rather than the members, and can be held responsible for violating those duties in running the company. The manager of a manager-managed LLC may be a founder who elected to set up the company that way or also can be selected by the members to manage. A manager-managed LLC may also be managed like a corporation, with a board of directors making the management decisions rather than a single manager. As you can see, the management flexibility of an LLC can be one of the advantages to choosing this business structure.

The members of an LLC typically contribute capital to the company in some form, whether it is cash, services, property, or an obligation to provide money or services in the future. Members also share in the profits and losses of the company based on their contribution to the company. An LLC can be structured in different ways, and typically this is set forth in the operating agreement of the company. The LLC can be managed equally by the members, or it can be manager-managed, where the company would be run more like a corporation with a board of directors, a CEO, or both. The management structure of the company must be specified in the articles of organization. From a liability standpoint, the LLC provides its members with protection from liability in that they are liable only for what they have contributed to the entity, and that their personal assets are not subject to attachment if a judgment is entered against the LLC.

In order to organize an LLC, as with a corporation, start by going to the secretary of state's website to obtain the Articles of Organization form. You will need to check what information and fees are required. The Articles of Organization typically ask for the following information:

- Name of the company
- Names and addresses of the members
- Name and address of the registered agent
- Designation of each member as either a member or manager
- Effective date

Like a corporation, the members of an LLC can face liability if a party suing the LLC is able to "pierce the veil" and show that members are not acting in accordance with the formalities of the company such that it is the alter ego of a member that results in harm to the company. Also like a corporation, once organized, the LLC must file an annual report with the secretary of state.

The governing of most LLCs is usually set forth in a document called an operating agreement. Like corporate bylaws, this document will address when the members and managers will meet, how decisions will be made on behalf of the LLC, how profits and losses will be shared, and other pertinent matters.

Now don't think if you choose a business entity that you are stuck with it forever. In many states it is possible to convert one business entity to another type if the need arises. There may be tax and other implications, so it is a good idea to consult your accountant and attorney if you are seeking to convert one entity to another.

» FUNDING

A critical concern for many start-up game companies is money, and for that reason we will now examine the different types of funding you can pursue and the benefits and drawbacks to them. Perhaps the most obvious type of funding is that from family and friends. This is perhaps the simplest way of finding funding, though depending on your network or family, it may not be the most fruitful funding source for your company. Another issue that can emerge with this type of funding is the potential awkwardness that can result at holiday parties and the like when Uncle Buck asks when you'll pay him back.

Another type of funding some companies pursue is that from "angel investors." Angels typically are wealthy individuals or groups of wealthy individuals who invest funds in start-up companies. True angel investors typically provide funding in the range of $10,000 to $50,000 to companies they feel have potential or have an interesting innovation. Finding an angel investor is typically done through colleagues, family, or friends. There are also angel investor clubs that fund start-ups. Angel investors vary in the amount of return that they want from an investment, and some can be similar in expectations to venture capital firms, but they still want to get a return on their investment. The process of getting funding through angel investors can be quicker than going the venture capital route, though you will still need to go through a vetting process before you get the money. Angel investors also vary in the amount of involvement they may expect, and if an investor is seeking more involvement in your business operations, it is a good idea to evaluate personalities as well as potential funding in making a decision to avoid potential conflicts in the future. Interviewing potential angel investors is also a good idea for start-ups to determine whether that particular angel is a good fit for the company. Obtaining angel investor funding can be more complex contractually, so it is a good idea to consult an attorney to assist you in setting up the arrangement between your company and angel investors.

A new category of potential investors that has developed is what are called "super angels." These investors typically provide funding in the range of $50,000 to $100,000 for individual investors, and $500,000 to $1 million collectively for early round funding. Super angels typically have several investments in different start-ups as part of their portfolio. The process of finding and pitching super angels is similar to that for true angel investors, though super angels may want to be more involved with your operations or may want a seat on your board of directors. While there has been quite a bit of activity on the angel investor front, there is some concern at the time of this writing that companies that received a first round of funding from angel investors may not be able to find a second round unless they can show a viable project.

Venture capital is another source of funding that is often sought. Venture capital firms will typically want a rate of return of 20 times their investment. One aspect of venture capital funding to keep in mind when pursuing it is that venture capitalists (VCs) typically will want to have some level of involvement in the company, which can mean a seat on the board of directors, a significant portion of ownership in the company, and appointment of one or more key personnel. If you are not a fan of giving up some level of control of your company, this may not be for you. However, VCs are also typically entrepreneurial, so if you find the right fit a venture capitalist can help your company grow and hopefully prosper. VCs may also be looking to bring in more experienced people to help the company or even to replace some of the existing leaders. However, depending on your personality this could be a good thing, as the company could grow beyond a level you feel comfortable managing, in which case replacing you or one of the founders as CEO could be a blessing rather than a problem. VCs also tend to be conservative in their approach to funding and business, which is good to keep in mind when preparing your pitch. Pursuing funding through venture capital also involves extensive vetting of your company and its finances, so having your books in order is important. The agreements involved with pursuing venture capital funding can be very complex and involved. It is best to consult an attorney licensed in your jurisdiction to help you draft the proper agreements and set up your company's stock offering and other matters so that they are in compliance with the Securities and Exchange Commission regulations.

A traditional source of funding in the game industry is financing available through the publisher. In these deals, a large publisher will contract with a developer for the development of a game. As part of the deal, the publisher will typically pay the developer an advance that is recoupable against future royalties from game sales, as well as payments for the completion of certain milestones of the game's development. The advantage of these types of deals is that a development company can get a large source of funding to develop a game, as well as the insight and guidance a publisher can provide. The drawbacks of publisher funding can include disagreements about whether a milestone has been met, which can cause delays in funding that can be problematic for developers on a tight budget, as well as possibly having to give up control of intellectual property or the company to the publisher.

A newer approach to funding video game development is completion bond financing, a concept that has been borrowed from the film industry. A development company using this type of financing would first typically obtain a publisher deal to develop a game, then take that promise by the publisher to pay for the development of the game to the bank to use as collateral for a bank loan. The game development company would then go to a bonding company that specializes in entertainment completion bonds to obtain a bond in case the game development company does not deliver the game. The bond acts as insurance for the game development company and provides it with money to repay the bank loan should that instance occur. In this type of financing, the bank, rather than the publisher, will pay the development company as it completes the milestones, which can mean more timely payments for the developer than in a publisher deal. The bonding company typically will charge a fee in the form of a percentage of the game's budget in return for providing the bond, and may require the development company to also put up collateral to secure the bond.

Another factor you need to consider in deciding what type of funding to pursue is the stage of development for your idea. How far along are you? Do you have a few animations as part of a sizzle reel or demo, or are you closer to having a fleshed-out prototype to show potential investors? Where are you in terms of your branding for your company?

Developing a Plan and a Pitch

An essential part of pursuing funding for your game company is developing a good pitch and business plan. Having a good plan and pitch for your company can make the difference between snagging an investor and missing out. It nearly goes without saying that in putting your business plan and presentation materials together, using good grammar and weeding out any typos are crucial. Investors, particularly venture capital firms, will expect a professional presentation and materials, and you want to put your best foot forward rather than have a glaring typo in your PowerPoint distract from a great pitch. It is also important to protect yourself and your company's intellectual property and plans by marking your business plan and materials as "confidential," as well as including a copyright notice such as "© 201_ (Your Company Name), all rights reserved" at the bottom of each page.

When putting together a business plan for investors, it is best to start your plan with an executive summary that sums up the essence of your plan in a few concise paragraphs. After that, start with a description of your concept and company that expresses your vision of what you want investors to see. Following that with a discussion of the strengths and weaknesses of your company or product after you have conducted the exercise below is the next logical step. Including a pro forma estimated income statement and budget as the next section is a good idea. In putting together this statement, it is best to be realistic about your potential financial needs, particularly if a milestone payment is not made on time. This often happens, especially when dealing with the bureaucracy of large publishers, and it can force you to consider cutting staff, office space, or equipment to survive the period of time until you get paid.

An exercise that can be particularly helpful in developing your pitch and in planning for marketing your game is what is called a SWOT analysis. This involves considering the strengths, weaknesses, opportunities, and threats in the market for your product or company. Having market research or data is beneficial to this process. Start with what you think are the strengths of your product, the traits that set it apart from other products and make it better than other games or components. Then look at what its weaknesses are, and what you can improve on. When pitching a product, you need to anticipate weaknesses potential investors may have concerns about so that you can address them if they come up in a meeting.

The next step is looking at the opportunities present in the market for your product. Is there a particular niche or demographic that is not being targeted that your product would fit into? Is there a current or developing trend that your product would fit into? Or perhaps there is a company looking for a product like yours to license or buy. Knowing what the business landscape is like for your product and company is important, and much as looking at the opportunities is important in developing a pitch, it is also crucial to understand the threats. Who is your competition for this product? Who are the big players in the market, and what type of products are they developing? Is there a big release coming that would impact sales of your product? Now while threats may seem like a bad thing, you can also look at them as a way of uncovering opportunities. A number of companies have benefited from turning what looked like a threat into an opportunity. If nothing else, this exercise will help you hone your pitch and marketing strategy for your game product.

Another good practice for developing your pitch is coming up with an "elevator speech." Imagine if you were on an elevator with your ideal pitch target—be it the CEO of a game publisher or a potential investor—and had only 30 seconds to pitch your product. You never know when an opportunity may arise at a trade show or other event, and having a short, engaging version of your pitch focused on the strengths and opportunities you identified can sometimes make the difference between making the deal and missing out.

Networking is also an important part of pursuing funding sources for your company. Joining professional game developer organizations is a good place to start. Attending conferences and events put on by these and other organizations is also helpful, not only in terms of information but also in providing networking opportunities. Use these opportunities to make contacts with people in the industry, and build relationships that potentially could help you find funding. If you're not the most outgoing person, networking can seem difficult at first, but if you don't talk to people about your company or game, who will? The Internet and social networking can also be great resources for spreading the word about your game. Setting up a Facebook page or a Twitter account to make announcements about your company and its products, as well as connect with fans, can be a powerful and relatively inexpensive way to build interest in your product.

3

BUSINESS RISK AND INSURANCE

By Sara Owens

Whether you consciously think about it or not, risk is something you face every day, both personally and professionally. It is how one chooses to deal with risk that will determine if the outcome is favorable or unfavorable. In this chapter risk will be defined and examined. By exploring some of the risks a start-up game developer may face you will begin to understand how your business might be affected by risk. You will see the importance of proactively addressing issues and building a plan of possible solutions that can be put in place to manage your risks. This chapter will provide you with some real-life examples of risks that have occurred in the game industry and a look at the potential outcomes game developers could have faced had the developers not managed their situations.

By the end of this chapter you should have the tools to be able to:

1. Identify some of the risks that your game development start-up company may face.
2. Understand the possible ways to manage your risks.
3. Create a basic outline to help determine the steps to take to address your risk.
4. Recognize the significance in consulting with professionals and experts in video game law and insurance.

Let's begin by defining risk. *Webster's* defines risk as:

1. possibility of loss or injury: peril
2. someone or something that creates or suggests a hazard
3. a. the chance of loss or the perils to the subject matter of an insurance contract; also: the degree of probability of such loss
   b. a person or thing that is a specified hazard to an insurer
   c. an insurance hazard from a specified cause or source

All businesses face risk. Game developers face many business risks unique to their start-up and situation. You should begin the process of evaluating your risk by making a list of what keeps you up at night. In other words what do you worry about within your company? What could go wrong and cause an interruption to the business? What could cause your business to fail or not get off the ground at all?

When these questions are posed to my game developer clients, here are just some of the risks my clients tell me they worry about:

- I worry about where my next project is coming from and whether it will come before I run out of money.
- What keeps me up at night is worrying about getting sued if I accidentally do something wrong and where we would get the money to pay for legal costs.
- I worry that I don't understand all of the details of the contract my publisher gave me.
- I worry that I will run out of money and the company will have to close its doors.
- Without question, my primary concern is making payroll for my employees and maintaining stability so that they can work hard and enjoy themselves without wondering whether their paycheck is coming. During these tough times, contracts are harder to come by and it takes a lot more effort on my part to secure them. It also takes a lot of patience and persistence to actually sign a contract, even after all terms have been negotiated and agreed upon. There are many factors outside of my control, which is why it keeps me up at night.

- What keeps me up at night is worrying about unknowingly and accidentally infringing on someone else's intellectual property. My guys would never do this on purpose but I worry that we might make a mistake.
- I worry the publisher will look for a reason not to pay us.

All of these are valid concerns that I have heard many times from my clients. Once you take the time to identify the risks you can move to the next step, determining a plan of how to manage those risks.

Now it is time for you to think of what causes you to lose sleep or what could potentially keep you up at night. Create a section of your business plan for risk management and insurance. If you do not have a business plan started at this time, grab a piece of paper and begin to create a list of potential perils your business could face. Be sure to keep this as a working document. This document should be revisited and revised regularly. As your game development company grows and changes so will the risks you face. Understanding these different risks as your business reaches new phases of development is the first step in mitigating them.

Once you have created a list of some of the things that you are concerned about within your business, you can start to develop a plan of action on how to deal with risk.

There are four basic ways to deal with risk: avoid risk, reduce risk, share/transfer risk, or accept risk. These four principles make up the framework for a term called enterprise risk management and they make up the structure that you will use to create a plan on how to address your risks. It is important to have a clear understanding of these principles in order to make the best choices for your business.

» AVOIDANCE OF RISK

First, let's begin by looking at the avoidance of risk. Avoidance means either not participating in or exiting the activities giving rise to risk. Think of avoidance this way: If you never drive a car you can never have a car accident. If you never develop a video game you can never be sued for breach of contract or intellectual property infringement. Avoidance may not be the most desirable or realistic way to manage all of your risk, but it is an option. This chapter won't spend a great deal of time on the concept of avoidance. Since you are reading this book about starting your own game development company you have to be willing to take on some risks. Starting any type of company involves risk and the video game industry presents some very specialized challenges. The key concept that you need to remember regarding the avoidance principle is that you cannot avoid all risks when starting a game company but you can avoid some of the risks. Here are just a few examples of risk that you should consider avoiding as a game development company:

1. Accepting unsolicited game ideas from people you don't know.
2. Hiring people to work for your company without having them complete an employment application even if they are your best friend or someone who is just going to be a contract employee.
3. Signing a contract before your legal team and insurance advisory have both reviewed it.
4. Working on a game for a publisher without a signed contract.
5. Using any content in your game that you do not have written consent from the content owner to use.
6. Taking the easy way out of a situation if you feel that the choice you are making could cause a potential problem for you in the future.

If the avoidance principle is not properly put into practice you might overuse the idea of avoidance and paralyze your company from ever getting started or if you ignore the principle altogether you could get into situations that could cripple your business and bring it to a grinding halt. It will be helpful for you to find the middle ground on avoidance. A basic guideline is to follow your instincts. Although that may not be the most profound advice, it is important for you as a business owner to trust what you know and make smart choices.

» REDUCTION OF RISK

The second principle of our framework, reduction of risk, is a more viable option for your start-up than the principle of avoidance. Reduction means taking action to minimize the likelihood or impact of a certain risk. By simply opening your doors, having employees or contractors working for you, or creating a game, you have risks that need to be managed. There are some very basic things that you can do to reduce your liability as a business owner. Below are just a few best practices that you should implement. As you are reading, think about how you can apply these concepts to reduce the risks you face in your business.

1. *Create an environment where it is safe for people to enter and work.* This may sound obvious but if your lead developer trips and falls on boxes or cables and ends up with a broken hand, you could end up with major delays and expenses that you did not expect. Simple steps can be taken to reduce this risk by keeping a neat work environment.
2. *Be sure that you are aware of all of the employment laws of your specific state.* As an employer it is your responsibility to know and follow the many business laws and employment and hiring practices. Failing to follow these rules and regulations can lead to fines and potential legal issues.
3. *Take the hiring and firing process seriously.* Know whom you are hiring. You are ultimately accountable for the work your employees and inde-

pendent contractors produce. Finding out what games and projects your employees or contractors have worked on in the past is a good barometer for what their work will be like.

4. *Check employee references.* Make sure your employees and contractors are signing confidentiality agreements and be sure you determine ahead of time who owns the intellectual property that is created while they are working for you.

5. *Read and understand the contracts between you and your publisher.* Oftentimes developers are so eager to get a contract in place that they will agree to just about anything. The dangers of signing a contract before you understand it could lead to significant hidden costs that can actually put you out of business. Some things to think about when looking at your contract include understanding how and when you will be paid so that you can set up a budget for cash flow purposes. Determine whether the time frame that is in place from your publisher is realistic. You don't want to be paying tons of overtime hours to your employees that you did not anticipate just so your milestones can be met.

6. *Understand what types of insurance, including the limits, you are required to obtain so that you can budget for those appropriately.* Contracts can be a daunting task and I highly recommend having an attorney who specializes in the game industry look at your contract before it is signed. No one likes to spend money on attorneys but it is important to not be penny-wise and pound-foolish. If you take a proactive approach and spend money on an attorney up front, you can save tremendous amounts of money and time later, as opposed to hiring an attorney when a problem arises once a contract is signed.

7. *Hire experts!* I mentioned hiring an attorney who specializes in the game industry and that holds true for the rest of the trusted advisors who are a part of your team. From your accountant to your insurance professional, seek out people who understand and are a part of your industry to help you grow your business.

If you are always taking a proactive approach to think through risks and create a plan, you will be ready if an issue occurs. It would be impossible for you to control every factor that might impact your business. That being said it is vital that you take action on the factors that are in your control and be prepared.

» INSURING OF RISK

The next concept in our framework is one that many people value as the most important principle of managing risk, and that is the transferring or insuring of risk. Sharing and insuring risk involves transferring a portion of risk most likely to a third party such as an insurance company, to reduce the amount of overall risk you might face. Insurance is a very effective and powerful way to transfer risk but it can be difficult to understand. What is covered and what is not covered? Every contract can be slightly different and the language can be confusing.

When I help my clients look at the best way to transfer their risk they often ask "Why do I need this insurance?" "What is really covered?" "Do I really need to spend money on insurance?" No one, including me, likes to spend money on something they hope to never use, and that is part of what insurance is at its core, spending money on something you hope to never use. One of the most important takeaways from this chapter that I want you to understand is what to look for when you are transferring your risk to an insurance company. Understand that not all insurance policies are created equal.

I spend a lot of my time analyzing insurance contracts for game developers and each contains different wording and nuances. Throughout this chapter I will outline four types of insurance that developers should have as part of their risk-management portfolio: general liability, business personal property, workers' compensation, and errors and omissions insurance. These four types of insurance do not make up a comprehensive list of all of the policies a developer needs but are some of the key policies you should have when you start your business. It is not uncommon to hear a developer say, "I want the cheapest insurance policy I can get." But if the cheapest policy you can get excludes source code or video games in general and is not going to pay at the time of a claim, why buy it at all? Not all insurance is created equal. It is always advised that you obtain errors and omissions insurance but you still need to consult an expert in video game insurance to help you find a policy that will meet your company's specific needs if there is a claim.

Let's take a step back and look at a general insurance example. Take automobile insurance, for instance. Everyone has to buy it, but I have never met anyone who said, "Boy, I hope I get to use my auto insurance today." But what if you do get into a car accident? Or what if someone steals your car? If that happens you would most likely put in a claim on your auto insurance policy and you would expect it to pay for the damage, right? But what if your policy's limits are too low and you can get only $500 for your car that is worth $25,000? Or what if you find out the auto insurance policy you bought covers every other car in the world but yours, so your claim will not be paid at all? Clearly I am exaggerating on these examples but you would be pretty upset if you were paying premiums, high or low, to an insurance company only to find out you don't really have the coverage you thought you did. You would expect to know before an accident that your car is covered for the amount you think it is insured for, and that there is coverage if you have an accident. The same is true for your business insurance. You want to make sure you know and understand the limits and what the insurance policy covers before you have a claim.

There is no way for me to say exactly what specific insurance policy or what precise limits you should have as a game developer without looking at the individual situation of your business. These unique factors will affect the cost of your insurance policy. However, there arc some general insurance guidelines that all game developers should look for in their insurance policies. It is important to note these are guidelines only and you should always consult a video game insurance professional for your specific situation.

1. *General Liability.* This type of insurance is something all companies regardless of industry should have as a part of their risk-management plan. An example of something a general liability policy would cover would be if a visitor in your office were to slip and fall and become injured. Another example of what should be covered under your general liability policy is products liability. It is important to make sure your scope of work as a video game developer is covered if a claim arises and it is equally important to know what your policy excludes. Some of the key elements that you must make sure are contained in the insurance policy you purchase are:
   a. Products liability
   b. Non-owned and hired auto
   c. Medical expenses
   d. Third-party product liability
   e. Tenant legal liability
2. *Business Personal Property and Business Income and Extra Expense.* It is important to make sure all of your business property is covered in case there is a covered loss. The key to this type of insurance is making sure you have accurate limits for your property and making sure you understand the types of losses the policy will cover. You need to do an inventory and make sure you know the value of all of the equipment that you have in your studio. Don't just pick a number out of the air. Everything from desks to the computers should be accounted for. Sometimes policies will have a sub or separate limit for computer and electronic equipment. This means that if you have a large amount of computer equipment it may not all be covered in a loss. Since most of the equipment in game development studios are computers or electronic equipment you need to make sure the appropriate limits are increased and the policy endorsed to include all of this property. Also, I mentioned understanding what a covered loss would mean. The policy will pay for a loss only if it is covered under the insuring agreement. For example if there is a loss because of a fire and fire is a covered loss the claim will be paid. However, if there is a loss due to an earthquake and your policy excludes earthquake coverage, any property that is damaged would not be covered because the earthquake is not a covered loss.
3. *Workers' Compensation.* Each state has different legal requirements for workers' compensation. You need to check with your state to see what you are legally obligated to obtain for your business. Some states require

you to buy workers' compensation insurance directly from the state while the majority allow you to buy workers' compensation insurance from a private insurance company. Many developers think that just because they do not have W2 employees and have only 1099 employees working for them that they are exempt from needing a workers' compensation policy. *This is not true.* I repeat. This is not true. Unless you, as a business owner, are going to require every independent contractor you hire to carry their own workers' compensation, and show you proof of that insurance policy, you need to obtain your own workers' compensation policy for your business. The ramifications for not having workers' compensation insurance can have a huge monetary impact including potential fines, medical costs, and future earned wages for an injured worker.

4. *Errors and Omissions Insurance.* This type of insurance is sometimes referred to as professional insurance. Errors and omissions is meant to cover a mistake that is made on a professional level that would have a financial impact. As a game developer it can be difficult to find an errors and omissions insurance policy to properly cover your unique business operations. Not every insurance company likes to insure game developers. Some of the key elements that you must make sure are contained in the insurance policy you purchase are:
   a. breach of contract coverage
   b. intellectual property rights infringement and source code
   c. defense costs
   d. worldwide coverage
   e. computer virus and hacking attacks
   f. third-party liability
   g. loss mitigation, defense costs, and settlement costs
   h. additional insured endorsement
   i. copyright, trademark, trade dress

Let's explore a little more in depth how errors and omissions coverage works in regards to IP infringement. If you are working on a concept for a game and someone comes along and says your game concept was her idea, you could be sued for stealing that idea. Even if you did not infringe or steal someone else's idea you are responsible to defend the accusation that has been brought upon you. Defending that sort of claim could be very costly in many ways. You could incur tremendous legal fees for your defense, and damage to your reputation, have to spend a significant amount of time away from your studio to get the situation under control, or worst of all, go out of business completely if you do not have enough resources to defend your claim. In this situation if you have an errors and omissions policy that covers your game company properly, you would have the ability to call on this policy to help you settle the claim, pay for your defense costs, and manage the overall situation.

Actual Claims Situations

You might be wondering what exactly would cause a claim and when you would have to use your insurance policies. There are many ways these policies could be triggered, from something as simple as the slip-and-fall example discussed under a general liability policy, to a complex situation of being accused of intellectual property infringement under an errors and omissions policy. You could face many potential claim situations.

Oftentimes developers will say these kinds of things don't really happen and insurance is just a rip-off. Although claims do not happen every day they can be expensive and catastrophic when they do occur. I want to share with you some real-life claims situations in the game industry and their financial impact. These examples are claims shared with me by actual insurance companies. Some of the details have been changed to protect the privacy of the client but the pertinent information on how the insurance policy played out is included. The first two examples deal with breach of contract situations and the last example deals with IP infringement.

1. In a recent large breach-of-contract dispute, a developer had contracted with a large U.S. publisher for delivery of a game based upon an original concept. It was a 36-month project with a total value to the developer of about $5 million. Throughout the development phase the publisher requested numerous changes to the game play as it was reacting to changes in the marketplace. Unfortunately there was not a clearly defined change control process within the contract and many of the changes were agreed either upon either verbally or by e-mail, often without full assessment of the implications for project delivery. Ultimately the game slipped past the due date and the developer was significantly over budget. It was also apparent that the publisher had lost desire for the game in question and was looking to escape the contract. Consequently a breach-of-contract notice was served on the developer. This dispute ran for over 12 months, during which period the errors and omissions policy footed the legal costs for the defense. Without this policy the developer would have had to face the situation alone and would have been unable to pay for the extensive legal fees that were incurred. Ultimately a settlement was reached that allowed the developer to re-sell the title to another publisher, thereby securing necessary funds to continue in business. I am confident in saying that without the proper insurance this company would be out of business today.

2. Another example where errors and omissions insurance came into play involved a developer who took over a failed project from another developer. It was a baseball game that had failed to deliver on the original specification. The insured agreed to fix all material bugs and get the game into a state where it would be approved by the publisher, a very large

U.S.-based publisher. Although this was achieved, the publisher failed to agree that the game was "fit for purpose" and it brought a breach-of-contract action. The insurance company defended the claim, using a specialist games law firm. Realizing that the developer had serious legal resources behind it, the publisher soon dropped the dispute on amounts due. The amount under dispute was only about $40,000 but without insurance this bill would have had to be entirely written off and the developer would have been on the hook for all of the legal fees.

3. The third example involves a European game developer that developed a game for a U.S. publisher. The publisher who marketed and distributed the game received notice of a claim that the games publisher infringed on its intellectual property rights (IPR) as the name and image used in the game had a strong likeness to its specific aircraft. The publisher sued the developers for breach of contract, due to the game-breaching IPR warranty. The insurance paid for an IT specialist, IPR game attorneys for defense, and ultimately a very large six-figure settlement.

It is critical to understand that risks are real and that not managing them properly could be detrimental to your business. You have now considered three examples and the reasons why you need to protect your business. But what if you do everything you can to manage risk, consult the experts, and put the proper insurance policies in place? Do risks still exist in your business? Of course they do. If you think back to the first principle in the framework you are reminded that the only way to eliminate risk completely is to avoid it all together. In order to have a business, you must face the fact that there will be risks, which brings us to acceptance, our last principle in the framework.

» ACCEPTANCE OF RISK

The last principle in the enterprise risk framework focuses on acceptance. Acceptance of risk is analyzing the situation and making an educated cost-benefit business decision to determine whether an action is worth taking. As you have learned in this chapter you can work to reduce risk by making smart business decisions, and you can transfer risk to an insurance company so that you are not faced with a major financial burden if there is a loss. But sometimes there are risks that you must accept as a cost of doing business. Maybe a risk is too costly to transfer, or maybe you have done everything correctly to minimize a risk, but the element of bad luck comes into play and you still have a loss. All businesses have limited funds at some point and a decision has to be made on what to spend that money on. In an ideal world you could insure or transfer all of your risk, but in reality the premium to insure every single risk would be far too expensive, so some risks need to be managed and simply accepted. A good example of this is patent risk.

Oftentimes the premium it would cost to insure a patent is so great, usually starting at a minimum of $25,000, that the patent owner will decide that the potential risk is something he or she is willing to take on as a cost of doing business. The most important element of accepting risk is deciding to take it on. You still need to recognize that you have a risk and you need to have an understanding of what that risk could mean to your business, both good and bad.

By now it is apparent that there are many risks your start-up game development company will face. These risks should not scare you but instead should empower you to properly protect your new business and all that you are building. At the end of this chapter (and on the attached CD) you will find a sample questionnaire that will help you consider the types of issues you will need to address to obtain proper insurance. If you review this document and remember the following key takeaways from this chapter you will be off to a good start as a prepared and successful business owner in game development.

1. Understand and create a list of what you worry about in terms of your business. You can't solve the problem if you don't know what it is!
2. Make sure you are always complying with the laws of your specific state especially as they relate to employment practices.
3. Read and understand the contract a publisher gives you.
4. Remember that not all insurance policies are created equal and cheaper is not better if your risks are not covered.
5. Rely on the experts. Find trusted advisors like attorneys, insurance professionals, accountants, and mentors who all have specialized experience in the game industry. Use them for advice, ask them lots of questions, and consult these people *before you sign a contract*!

Game Guard Insurance ™ Questionnaire

This questionnaire is meant as a basis to begin the insurance application process. Additional documentation will be required to obtain formal quotes. This form is proprietary and may not be replicated without the written consent of Game Guard Insurance ™ .

Company Name: _____

Address: _____

_____

Phone: _____

Email: _____

Contact Person and Title: _____

1. Do you plan to begin developing a video game within the next 24 months?

2. Do you have any employees (including 1099s)? If yes, how many?

3. Do you use a third party for any game or content development?

4. Do you have contracts in place with all third-party developers?

5. Do you have appropriate legal counsel review all contracts before they are signed? If yes, who?

6. Do you always have signed contracts in place with a publisher before you begin working on a game?

7. Do you accept unsolicited game ideas?

8. Do you have a contract that requires you to carry specific limits for General Liability and Errors and Omissions Insurance? If yes, please list the limits required and attach a copy of the contract:

Describe your Business Operations:

List any Games you have worked on in the past 5 years, including titles, dates of work, and revenue:

List your company revenues and revenue projections:

Previous Year Revenue	
Current Year Projected Revenue	
Next Year Projected Revenue	

Describe the projects you are currently working on:

Signature: _____

4

INTELLECTUAL PROPERTY AGREEMENTS

By Shawn Gorman

"The last thing you want in a business relationship in this business is to have only a handshake agreement. Always follow up with a robust contract. A skimpy contract that doesn't spell out everything to your satisfaction gives the stronger partner way too much leverage. Not being anal is a mistake that every first-time developer makes."

— *Ted Price, CEO, Insomniac Games*

» INTRODUCTION

I recently received an inquiry from a developer looking to protect a new software concept. The idea was brilliant and it was clear that the developer was bright and had done his homework on obtaining a patent. For a patent attorney, this was the perfect client. Unfortunately, however, this young, bright developer was misinformed regarding one issue. Specifically, he was led to believe that the sole issue for intellectual property protection was whether he should apply for a patent. As a patent attorney, I did not dispute the importance of obtaining adequate patent rights. I did, however, explain that obtaining patent protection, by itself and without closely considering contractual issues, would likely benefit his competitors (or soon-to-be competitors) to his detriment.

The conversation immediately focused on agreements. We had to discuss whether his employer had any rights in the invention, whether there were other inventors, and if so, what agreements had been reached. That conversation led to whether he had spoken with any third parties, including friends or family, regarding his idea, and if so, whether he obtained a confidentiality agreement. Discussions regarding agreements did not end there—we discussed whether he would want to sell and/or license any rights he may have in the invention. Needless to say, the developer left our conversation with more homework, but he was very thankful we discussed these issues before filing any patent applications. These same issues apply to all video game developers, whether they are large entities or sole developers trying to determine whether to start their own ventures.

In short, it is futile to spend several thousand dollars obtaining a patent (or any other form of intellectual property protection) that is utterly useless without the proper agreements in place. This chapter aims to convey the importance of agreements, both from an offensive and defensive position. Agreements should not be seen as an alternative to other forms of protection. Rather, without agreements other forms of protection may not be available.

The scope of IP agreements has been the topic of many rather large books, which are often broken into several volumes. A single chapter, therefore, cannot encompass every possible IP agreement that you will encounter. This chapter is intended to provide guidance on the questions that need to be asked and issues that need to be addressed when working with these agreements. By explaining the rationale for drafting agreements and certain language for consideration, you will be more prepared to speak with your attorney about several types of IP agreements. In this regard, this chapter explains various issues in the context of a specific type of agreement; however the same issues are very likely important for other types of agreements. For example, the ownership of new inventions is a serious issue for both a nondisclosure agreement as well as an employment agreement. Therefore, understanding these issues is likely to be more useful for your success than providing several volumes of exemplary agreements that you don't have the time to review.

The Sooner the Better

Luckily, the bright developer referenced above spoke with counsel before investing time and money in his concept. Unfortunately, some initial consultations with developers and gaming clients do not end the same way. Receiving a referral or a cold call from an excited developer who recently applied for a patent (and/or blogged about the concept) can be a difficult conversation. Imagine telling someone who cashed in his retirement account or quit his job to start a new video game venture that he forfeited his ability to protect his idea or that his competitor can exploit his idea without compensation. Luckily, most developers come to us early enough for us to minimize any past damage and to obtain the best protection we can—whether it be patent, trademark, copyright, and/or trade-secret based. Still, we'd like to make sure more developers are able to protect various aspects of their hard work. If there is one central dogma to agreements, it is this: the sooner the better.

It is *never* too soon to consider agreements. The sooner you consider agreement-related issues, the more likely you can avoid inescapable situations and unnecessary legal fees down the road. As you know, developing video games requires multiple parties from diverse backgrounds both in the form of personal relationships as well as business relationships with previously unknown corporate entities. Agreements provide a great avenue to ensure everyone knows the rules up front, before things get complicated. As stated previously, just like good fences makes good neighbors, good contracts make good business partners.

No Developer Is an Island

You, either alone or perhaps with your trusted co-developer, have spent (or will spend) countless hours conceiving and/or coding your idea into reality. You may start believing that you are an island. After all, you conceived of the idea, coded the concepts, and maybe even started testing them—likely over late nights when the rest of the world was sleeping. You rightfully form a strong bond with the work. Because others' involvement is rather small in terms of time, money, and risk, you may forget about this involvement. Nonetheless, for most situations, multiple other parties have been involved. Neglecting to account for this involvement is the Achilles' heel of this stage of development.

Think about the "aha moment" when you first conceived of the idea for your game. Your initial reaction to the "aha moment" may have been to tell your business partner or even a friend the news. You may have wanted some basic feedback or even hoped someone would tell you that it was the greatest idea that they ever heard. Immediately, agreements come to mind. Did that person make a suggestion that, although it may have been common sense, is incorporated into your code? Will you beta-test? If so, will you allow blogging about the product to build recognition among potential customers or production companies? The initial stage of development is the most exciting time—ideas are flying back and forth, people are excited, plans are being made. Unfortunately, it's also one of the most dangerous times for developers. It's dangerous because everyone—yes, everyone—has different interests and understandings of what their roles are. Further, the mere act of telling another person may prevent obtaining a patent or retaining other rights in an idea, an expression of that idea, or subsequent derivations. Thus, agreements are likely needed in more situations than you may initially realize.

» NONDISCLOSURE AGREEMENTS

Overview

A nondisclosure agreement (NDA) is perhaps one of the most important items in a developer's arsenal. Similar to a shopkeeper selecting which brands to market, which distributors to use, and how to lock up the store at night, a developer has to consider how to best create and protect his or her ideas—from conception through the final product. When properly used, NDAs may provide the much-needed time required to refine your idea, reduce the likelihood of a competitor capturing your idea, or even prevent another party from benefiting from your prior expertise, such as by utilizing your disclosure without compensation. From the "aha moment" onward, developers should always ask: Do I need an NDA with this person or entity? Before going into nondisclosure agreements, it's worth examining why they are such valuable tools.

Friends and Family—Not Just for Calling Plans

Before jumping into various aspects of NDAs, it's worthwhile to consider a touchy subject—the subject of "friends" and family. We surround ourselves with people we trust. Whether it's a trusted developer or a partner in the software field, there is at least one person that you "trust" with helping you foster the company's ideas and expressions of ideas. I find that the same is true regardless of whether the gaming client is part of a large entity or a small group of developers. Even at Fortune 250 companies, individuals have someone, perhaps even working for another entity, whom they reach out to for general advice. It may be someone they want to work with to further develop the company's ideas. In fact, the person may have helped the company in the past, and either the developer or the executive team desires to work with them in the future. Clearly, this person can be trusted and asking them to sign an agreement saying they are trustworthy is insulting, right? Here comes the bad news . . . from an agreement perspective, you may have to treat them as if they are not a friend or family member. This may sound impersonal and a bit impractical at first. When I first started advising clients, I wondered whether they thought I was crazy. It was not long before I got my answer. A gentleman and founder of a gaming company, who turned out to be a long-time client, was the first one who bluntly told me in so many words that I was crazy. I realized from that conversation and several others that providing some legal background before launching into the statement often resulted in the client ensuring that everyone signed an NDA, even those that may not have been needed. So here is the ugly truth—the law does not care about personal distinctions between trusted advisors and fierce competitors.

The law does not care if Nintendo®, Sony®, and Microsoft® are best friends or competitors when deciding whether a disclosure is public or confidential. In this regard, assume you develop a novel gaming environment for *Snowdown*. Whether you can obtain a patent to protect this gaming environment may boil down to whether you publicly disclosed these concepts. Implications of this will also be discussed later.

Further, a central theme throughout this chapter is that agreements ensure everyone is on the same page before things get complicated. Does everyone agree about all the following: Ownership (including possible new or derivative works)? Compensation? Time line? A colleague at another company may have the best intentions to devote his company's resources to work on the *Snowdown* idea; however, he may get promoted—either internally or externally—and in the blink of an eye, you are working with someone who might not like the project or might, without realizing it, inadvertently disclose confidential information to a third party.

One Size Does Not Fit All

A quick web-based search will provide thousands of basic NDA templates. An example of a basic NDA is also provided on the attached CD. Very rarely would I recommend using someone else's template. There is almost always at least one important issue that a client needs to cling to. Below are some issues that need to be considered for each NDA you provide to a different entity or individual. This list is not exhaustive; rather it's meant to provide examples of some issues and concepts for which you should consult your attorney about whether to include within an agreement.

Scope and the Flow of Information

What is the purpose of the relationship? It's a basic question, but it's often overlooked. Let's think about the question in the following two scenarios:

Scenario #1:
A video game developer wishes to meet a production company to discuss a new concept for *Snowdown* in hopes of producing *Snowdown* for all of the popular gaming platforms.

Scenario #2:
A video game developer has written the *Snowdown* software for a new gaming platform and a separate hardware company invented and developed a new controller. Both parties are interested in ensuring the controller works with the video game platform before the controller or the platform is publicly available.

Using the same NDA for these two scenarios would likely lead to disastrous results. Looking first to Scenario #1, what is the purpose of the agreement? Well, the developer may want the production company to fund the project and/or provide expertise in finalizing the project. As the developer, you should ask: Who needs confidential information to fulfill the purpose of the relationship? In this case, the production company may need your information to determine whether to invest the money or to adequately determine a budget to fulfill its obligation. Next determine whether you really need or want the other side's information. The developer may want to provide the production company with a "one-way" NDA such that it covers only confidential information provided to the production company but does not cover any information provided by the production company. This may seem counterintuitive at first. After all, wouldn't that encourage more open discussion? It may, but it also opens up liability to the developer. Further, as discussed later in this chapter, exchange of information is often accompanied by obligations—and lots of them—for example, obligations regarding how to store, transmit, utilize, mark, and potentially destroy or account for information following termination of the NDA.

One-Way NDA

Always consider the cost-benefit analysis of obtaining another entity's information. In this regard, there are risks for obtaining unwarranted information, even if the information may be relevant. Presume, for example, that both parties mutually agree not to disclose (or conduct unauthorized uses with) the other's confidential information in advance of a meeting to discuss *Snowdown*. During the meeting, the production company shares its ideas of further concepts for additional online games—ideas that would be perfect for *Snowdown II* or another game you are working on. Your company is now contaminated. It does not take much imagination to understand the difficulty the developer may face if he wishes to independently pursue a similar concept, even if that developer already pursued preliminary work on that concept. It would be very difficult explaining to a third party—such as an arbitrator, judge, or jury—that you really did independently have these ideas after receiving background or similar information from the other party. Further, now the developer must review all the incoming information, determine who can review it, and enforce restrictions on its storage and access. For example, can more than one copy be printed out? Must it be destroyed? This could lead to a lot of unneeded headaches. Therefore, you may wish to expressly declare neither you nor your company desires to receive certain information and, more important, that there is no obligation in regard to protecting their information from disclosure. Such language might include portions of the following:

> Since it is not [DEVELOPER'S] desire to be afforded access to any of [COMPETITOR'S] or a third party's Proprietary Information, [COMPETITOR] agrees that receipt by [DEVELOPER] of any information from [COMPETITOR] shall not impose any confidentiality

obligations on [DEVELOPER], and [COMPETITOR] shall not be liable for any use or disclosure that it makes of such information. [COMPETITOR] agrees to refrain from disclosing any information to [DEVELOPER] that [COMPETITOR] knows, or has reason to know, infringes on any trade secret or other property right of any third party.

The second question is how you should limit the production company's use of this information. Think of all the legal actions it could perform with that information while still not technically disclosing that information. Thus, if you are providing the confidential information, you want the scope of the NDA to be narrow. Alternatively, if you are receiving the information, you would generally prefer a broader scope to prevent accusations of improperly using the information. Some language for setting forth the scope of a one-way NDA may include the following passage:

> The Confidential Information being disclosed under this Agreement is to be used solely for the purpose of discussions, testing, and analyzing [DISCLOSER'S] methods and systems relating to [DESCRIPTION OF *SNOWDOWN'S* NOVEL FEATURES] (the "Purpose").

However, be sure to tell your attorney everything about your specific situation so he or she can best counsel you.

Two-Way NDA

One-way NDAs are not a panacea. There are many situations in which both parties need access to the other's information to adequately fulfill the intended goals of the parties. For example, looking to Scenario #2 above, the video game developer will likely need access to the confidential controller to modify or tweak the code of *Snowdown* and/or test the controller with the new platform. Likewise, the hardware developer may need source code or other confidential information to ensure that the controller properly interfaces with the platform to provide a successful user experience when playing *Snowdown*. You want to ensure the other side properly safeguards this information. This is especially true when working with large production or platform companies that work with several different developers.

Whether I represent a large multinational corporation or an individual, I find that people enter agreements with the best intentions. People enter agreements to benefit each other. Unfortunately, however, the person who signed the agreement with you might not be the person ensuring compliance with it or who is acting on that information on a daily basis. It's not that the production company is out to intentionally harm you, but often your contract or business relationship is categorized based upon what the agreement says—is it a one-way or a two-way

NDA? What is the scope? Thus, certain obligations may be mapped to a binary entry in a spreadsheet (e.g., 0=yes, 1=no). This mapping may be transmitted to another individual in the company who needs to act on that information as part of his or her job. Thus, if you supply a company with confidential information without restrictions, you essentially have given it the right to exploit that information for any and all purposes. That company may have already been working on something similar and you've just given them other items to consider. In essence, you've eliminated the need to continue working with you. Spend the few extra minutes to determine how you want your information used.

Confidential, Proprietary, or Both

What Are We Talking About?

We have referred to this hypothetical "confidential" information, but we haven't really set forth what it is. Clearly, everything you provide a third party is not confidential and you can bet that they would not sign an agreement stating otherwise. Your NDA needs to set forth what is confidential. Is it certain information regarding the code of *Snowdown* or is it much broader, such as new concepts for player interaction? Defining confidential information may be done a variety of ways. Again, like many of these issues, your preference is influenced by your position.

If you are disclosing information, you may wish to recite a blanket statement that covers any information that the other party receives with narrow exceptions for information that is clearly publicly known. One example of a blanket statement may include:

> "Confidential Information" as used in this Agreement means any and all information disclosed to or otherwise obtained by the Recipient from [DEVELOPER] in the course of performance of this Agreement, whether in writing, orally, visually, or by samples. Without limitation, this shall include . . .

If you plan to disclose unpublished patent applications, you may recite the application numbers in this section. This will ensure that you can freely discuss the novel features of the invention. Such blanket statements followed by exceptions are very common; however, if you are receiving the information, you may consider ensuring that the scope of "Confidential Information" is narrowly defined, such as limited to the subject matter of a patent application relating to a video game console's controller. Be cautious, however, of trapping yourself.

How Will We Know?

Of course, if you are receiving this information, do you really want to decipher each and every piece of received information to determine whether it's confidential? You may want to require that the other side expressly mark confidential information as "CONFIDENTIAL." Conversely, they may want you to agree that if confidential information is not marked as such, but you knew (or should have known) it is confidential, then you cannot disclose it or use it outside the scope of the agreement just because it was not properly marked. Obviously marked materials are easier to work with, but do both parties have the time and resources to categorize and mark each document that contains valuable information?

Proprietary Information

You may have information that does not neatly fit into the "confidential" category, but nonetheless, you do not want the other side to be able to exploit it. Therefore, you may wish for your NDA to recite what, if any, information you believe to be proprietary, and what restrictions need to be placed on that information. In some instances, you may want it treated like confidential information, yet in others, you may not.

Don't Get Left in the Dark

Technology moves fast. Yesterday's latest and greatest idea will be in tomorrow's discount bin. Should your agreement set forth who owns further co-developed ideas? A few years ago, most parties initially objected to this as being "premature" at this stage. I was negotiating an NDA for a gambling client when the attorney for the other company abruptly said that his client would not consider signing such a premature agreement. After I asked two simple questions, the other side was eager to discuss these provisions. The first question was: Is it possible that an employee of his client could co-invent a concept with my client during their discussions? He answered yes, and then I simply asked: "And you know that under U.S. laws, absent an agreement to assign their rights, each inventor has an undivided right to exploit their invention?" He then realized that leaving out that provision would essentially allow my client to exploit any new ideas without compensation. Needless to say, the agreement included the relevant provisions.

Who Owns the New Stuff?

I did not push the issue to provide the other side an upper hand, but rather it was just as probable that my client could have co-invented an idea that could be exploited by either side without compensation. The other side had more manufacturing capabilities than my client, so it was in my client's interest to ensure that provision was in the contract to prevent them from mass-producing products with these ideas. This is not to say that you will always be on the benefiting side of this provision, but in general, predicting the outcome of brainstorming sessions is futile. Therefore, it's akin to gambling when you don't at least consider discussing this provision.

Developers generally agree that subsequent rights for co-discoveries should be fairly apportioned. Raising this provision with the other side also shows that you are being fair and want both sides to benefit from the relationship. Unfortunately, this provision still requires some forethought. First, let's assume that we live in a perfect world in which developers, designers, production companies, distributors, and component manufacturer live in harmony. You execute an NDA with a production company and you co-develop a concept that is very beneficial to each side. You may rightly believe that you should own 90 percent of the rights of the idea, while they believe they own 50 percent of it. For example, using Scenario #1 above as an example, you sign an NDA with the hardware company in advance of a meeting to discuss the new online game. The discussion turns to subject matter that technically is partially outside the scope of the agreement. Alternatively, the other entity may believe that it should own 100 percent of ideas that relate more closely with its business and that you should keep any rights to ideas that are more closely aligned with your business. Alternatively, it may feel entitled to a lion's share of the profits if its equipment was used, even if you contributed more "intellectual capital." Therefore, it's best to air out these issues before getting into a relationship. At the very least, the parties should agree to work in good faith to resolve such issues. As part of these and other transfer-of-rights issues, you may need to include provisions of assignments, work for hire, etc. These concepts will be explained in more detail below in relation to employment agreements.

» EMPLOYMENT AGREEMENTS

Introduction

Regardless of how "small" you may believe a project is, chances are that you would greatly benefit from some sort of employment agreement. The term "employment agreement" is being used rather loosely. Many of the issues discussed below equally apply to retaining individuals or other companies for various reasons, such as for conducting research and development.

There are a lot of issues to consider, and as you know, not all of them are legal in nature. Depending on the specific niche, you may have to compete with well-funded competitors who can offer generous perks. Losing a great mind over a single clause in an agreement would be a shame. Alternatively, paying people to develop their own ideas on your dime is just as bad. This is true regardless of whether you are the largest software developer in the world or just a start-up.

Define Your Culture

Whether you are a developer hiring an employee or the developer being hired, you should utilize an employment agreement as both a training opportunity as well as a marketing tool. It cannot be emphasized enough that agreements provide a great avenue to ensure that everyone knows the rules up front. In this regard, employees, for the most part, want to do great work. An employee hired to help create Bella's character does not start the job with an intention of producing a lackluster character. He or she will often take a personal pride in his or her characters. A well-crafted employment agreement can be used to indicate your company's willingness to foster a culture that rewards and retains great programmers and other integral employees. Use caution, however, because an overly liberal agreement may encourage the improper dissemination of your intellectual property as well as invite suits from other competitors.

Conversely, an overly restrictive agreement could result in a poor reputation among skilled candidates resulting in long-term problems in attracting or retaining candidates. In this regard, proper training used in conjunction with the employment agreement can set forth the importance of 1) dealing with others' intellectual property, 2) nondisclosure of information, and 3) addressing other client-specific concerns. The agreement can then be used as a last resort if an employee jeopardizes the company's future by refusing to follow the rules.

Protecting Third-Party Rights

As odd as it seems, part of the agreement actually serves to protect your competitor's information. Before diving into this topic, let's go back to the decision to hire this employee. You hired this individual for a reason. You (or someone at your company) can identify a quality that this employee had over other candidates. Chances are this quality related to the person's experience or higher levels of creativity or intelligence. Therefore, you can readily imagine that a prior employer may have also liked that same quality and attempted to best utilize it at that company. In fact, unless every employee is hired right out of school, chances are that they have been "contaminated" with someone's confidential or proprietary information.

Luckily, the mere possession of another's trade secrets is not a reason not to hire an individual. In fact, most potential candidates have been exposed to some sort of information. You should, however, confirm that knowledge of that information is not directly correlated to the person's role within your entity such that you would improperly benefit from another's trade secrets or similar information. Thus, an agreement may request that the employee warrant he or she is not violating any agreements or obligations. For example:

> Employee warrants that he/she is not subject to any agreements or obligations to others that would interfere in any way with employment by the Company and his/her responsibilities to the Company as stated in this Agreement and otherwise. Employee agrees not to disclose to the Company or use in connection with his/her employment by the Company any Proprietary Information belonging to a third party.

Protecting Your Intellectual Property

You likely didn't hire the employee to squander your resources without producing something valuable. Instead, you likely hired this person to outsmart and out-create the employees of your competitor. In this regard, it is important to determine up front what each party's expectations are. Are you hiring the employee to create specific materials? Will the employee retain any rights to the created materials? Will extra compensation be provided for additional materials or innovation? Regardless of what the arrangement is, it's important to understand the laws regarding inventorship, ownership, and assignment of the various types of intellectual property. In this regard, many U.S. rights, including patents and copyrights, vest in the individual inventor, not in the employer. Without an agreement to the contrary, your employees may very well own any patents and/or copyrights developed during working hours.

Work for Hire

Assuming you are hiring an employee to write code for the *Snowdown* game, you will need to familiarize yourself with the "work for hire" doctrine of copyright laws. Software code, in itself, is protectable by copyright law (certain functional outcomes of executing the code may further be protected by other forms of IP, such as utility patents). Absent any agreement to the contrary, the author of the code or any other "expression on a tangible medium" is the owner. Obviously, in today's information age, it hardly seems fair that a developer hired to create an expression—such as the specific look of the character Bella or Bolt—owns the rights to that expression. The work for hire doctrine recognizes that employees often create items for their employers. In essence, they are hired to create works. Indeed, anything created by an employee in the ordinary course of his or her employment is actually a work made for hire and ownership automatically passes through to the employer. However, it never hurts to include a blanket statement in your agreement that all work (especially code) is a "work for hire" for which you or your company is the author, to the extent the law does not already achieve that result.

As one example, you may wish to first set forth what qualifies as a work for hire and then set forth the arrangement of ownership. One example may include:

> The term "Work for Hire" means all original works of authorship that are made by [EMPLOYEE] (solely or jointly with others) within the scope of the Purpose and that are protectable by copyright pursuant to United States Copyright Act (17 U.S.C. §101) and/or the copyright laws (or equivalent or similar laws) of other jurisdictions.
>
> [EMPLOYEE] acknowledges and agrees that any and all work product created in the course of performing Services, whether performed by [EMPLOYEE] alone or with other employees, agents,

contractors, personnel, or any third party working on behalf of or under contract with [EMPLOYER] is a Work for Hire of which [EMPLOYER] is the author.

There are some types of work, however, that may not be transferred as a work for hire. Further, as the economy becomes global, it's important to remember that not all development may occur within the United States, and therefore, may not be considered a work for hire. Therefore, you want to consider whether to ensure ownership is properly transferred to you or your company.

An exemplary clause may include:

> To the extent that any such work product:
>
> i) is prohibited by law or regulation from being a Work for Hire of which [EMPLOYEE] is the author, or
>
> ii) is for any other reason not deemed a Work for Hire of which [EMPLOYEE] is the author,
>
> [EMPLOYEE] hereby assigns, conveys, transfers, and agrees to assign, convey, and transfer all rights and title in the work product to [DEVELOPER] provided, however, that if such assignment, conveyance, or transfer is prohibited by law or regulation, [EMPLOYEE] hereby grants and agrees to grant to [DEVELOPER] an exclusive, paid-in-full, non–royalty-bearing, sublicensable worldwide license to use such work product as if it were owned by [DEVELOPER] without lien or encumbrance.
>
> i) Under any assignment, conveyance, or transfer of ownership and title from [EMPLOYEE] to [DEVELOPER], [DEVELOPER] shall retain a nonexclusive, worldwide, revocable, non–royalty-bearing, sublicensable right and license in the New Developments assigned, conveyed, or transferred to utilize the work product for the Purpose of this Agreement.

Likewise, employment agreements as well as other agreements, such as nondisclosure agreements, may include clarification that "Works for Hire are considered within the scope of New Developments." In addition, always include both an assignment clause and a work for hire clause every agreement with independent contractors—they're not employees and thus not subject to the same work for hire pass-through mentioned above.

Assistance

I am veering off topic slightly to address a related issue that I think is very worthwhile to discuss and will affect the costs of obtaining intellectual property protection for your company. As immediately discussed above, you likely will have rights "assigned" to you or your company in some form or another. In this regard, spend time seriously considering whether you will reward employees based upon the generated intellectual property. Rewards can be based upon the number of disclosures, applications filed, patents granted, or a variant that combines several of these. Yet, other entities choose not to reward employees based upon specific rights granted, but rather use traditional review processes to determine how to compensate their employees. Each has its merits and drawbacks. The boxed section at the end of this chapter, IP Reward Programs, will briefly discuss some approaches that may be modified to suit your needs. For now, however, keep in mind that a reward system may increase cooperation from employees in harvesting new ideas as well as securing rights for those ideas.

You will need cooperation and assistance from your employees to adequately secure IP rights. Agreeing to assign rights to you is different from "playing nicely" in doing so. Further, even the best-intentioned employees may leave the company and be difficult to convince once working for your competitor. Therefore, your agreement should include a section that requires the employee to undertake certain activities that are required to secure your rights. One example may require employees to:

> do all lawful things necessary to ensure the Company's ownership of such New Developments, including without limitation the transferring to the Company and its assigns all of the Employee's rights, title and interest in and to such New Developments, and the rendering of assistance in execution of all necessary documents required to enable the Company to pursue and obtain Proprietary Rights in the United States and foreign countries on any of such New Developments.

As discussed below, further provisions may provide guidance on other ways an employee can assist in preserving your intellectual property rights.

Morally Speaking

Even if an author assigned ownership of the "work" to you, that person may still have "moral rights." Moral rights allow the author to still be identified as the author and possibly to be able to create and retain ownership to derivative works. Thus, consider whether you want to allow employees to have these rights or at least a subset of them.

These are also important considerations for the employer to consider in its dealings with third parties. For example, suppose *Snowdown* is a hit and you are invited to write an article for a magazine. You may want to retain rights to publish the article on your website or pass it out at a trade show. What if an online video review would make a great marketing tool? Can you use it? If so, how can you use it? Thus, determining rights of ownership and moral rights is an important consideration.

Moral rights vary by country, and in the United States they are limited to works of visual art, which exclude works made for hire. So moral rights really come into play only when you take ownership by assignment of a copyrighted work of fine art such as a painting, drawing, print, sculpture, or photograph that exists only as an original or that is limited to no more than 200 signed and numbered copies.

Is It Too Late?

If reading this chapter has you a bit worried about your current agreements or lack of agreements, there is some potentially good news. Many jurisdictions have a shop right doctrine. Generally, if an employee invents something while conducting activities within the scope of his or her employment or otherwise utilizes the company's resources, then the company may have a shop right to exploit the rights in it. Thus, if an employee creates a new process that is unrelated to the development of *Snowdown* during his or her employment using company resources, your company may have a shop right to utilize that process in the release of *Snowdown* or other business activities, but you should check with an attorney to be sure. There are two important considerations, however, that limit shop rights: 1) you can't prevent the inventor/author from licensing or selling his or her rights to your competitor; and 2) you can't sell or license your rights except as part of a sale of the entire company. Further, the shop right doctrine generally applies to patent law and is not typically extended to copyright law, which generally would be governed only by the work for hire doctrine.

Therefore, it's generally recommended that you ask existing employees to execute a new employment agreement. This will allow you to ensure that your arrangement with your developers is up to date and in line with your intellectual property strategy. However, the premise of an employment agreement is that you generally agree to provide a benefit (e.g., the job with a paycheck) for something in return (e.g., assignment of IP rights). Well, if they already have that paycheck, the agreement may need to offer them something else. In most jurisdictions, merely keeping them at that job is not deemed a new benefit. So, for these individuals, provide them with a bonus. It can be pretty low, such as $10 or so, but make sure they get a benefit from signing the agreement. Because individual jurisdictions enforce these sections differently, it does not hurt to recite each of the benefits (consideration) the employee is receiving. One example may include the following recitation:

> In consideration of [Company's] agreement to employ or continue to employ [Employee], wherein it is understood that such employment may be terminated at will of the [Company], and in further consideration, independently sufficient, of providing [Employee] immediate and/or future access to [Confidential Information, etc.] and the remuneration now and hereafter paid to Employee, and in further consideration, independently sufficient, of the currently awarded remuneration, [a payment of $$$ (and/or) promotion to

XXX], and in further consideration, independently sufficient, of any future promotion(s) awarded to Employee and/or bonus(es) paid to Employee [possible other consideration], and for other good and independently sufficient consideration, the receipt and sufficiency of which are hereby acknowledged by each of the Parties hereto, the Parties hereto agree as follows. . . .

Don't Throw Away the Rights

External Disclosure

For both the employer and the employee to benefit from the innovation, their actions must be coordinated to ensure their actions don't jeopardize your ability to capture the intellectual property stemming from the innovation. If you intend to preserve certain innovations as trade secrets then you want to ensure certain procedures are in place to prevent loss of the secrets to the public domain. The same applies to patentable innovations. For example, most jurisdictions outside of the United States require "absolute novelty." Thus, any nonconfidential disclosure bars obtaining foreign rights. Even the United States grants only a limited one-year grace period following disclosure to file for patent protection. In short, filing a patent application is a "limited time offer."

```
Why are the laws so strict in regard to public disclo-
sure? Video game developers rightfully question the strict
disclosure rules. For example, it takes time to determine
whether a concept is patentable. Then, unless you work in a
fantasy world in which you can print unlimited cash, devel-
opers must prioritize which, if any, concepts to proceed
with. Even after deciding to seek protection, there are
serious cost and time demands to properly prepare and file
patent applications, which are complex legal and technical
documents. A lot of questions need to be answered in a rel-
atively short period of time. And this is just looking at
the IP rights. A frustrated co-founder of a start-up once
bluntly asked: "Doesn't the government understand that I am
simultaneously meeting with investors, hiring employees,
and evaluating the overall feasibility of the business con-
cept?" Needless to say, the laws can be unforgiving.

    So why are the laws so unforgiving? Well, the patent
system was designed to promote innovation by rewarding
the inventor(s) for a limited time in exchange for fully
disclosing the invention so that after the limited time
of protection, society as a whole may freely utilize
(and hopefully further refine and improve on) the inven-
tion. Thus, there needs to be a discrete starting point
from which to measure the limited time. While not everyone
```

agrees with the implementation, the laws were designed to
encourage the prompt disclosure of these ideas and prevent
an unfair extension of the patent right. To fully understand this, imagine being a competitor of *Snowdown*'s developer. *Snowdown*, by the way, is the new hit video game that
every kid, teenager, and adult wants. It's that good. You
may have a competing product that is two months away from
release. What do you do? Would it be fair for *Snowdown*'s
developer to wait until you release your product and then
be able to file for protection several years down the line
and sue you for past infringement? No. Such laws would not
provide the needed stability to encourage innovation. Thus,
current laws attempt to encourage a prompt decision whether
to retain inventions as a trade secret or file for protection and fully disclose the idea for public inspection.
Whether the time restraints perfectly achieve that balance
may be up for debate, but it's something that your agreements need to take into account.

Therefore, it may be worth considering a clause that requires employees to either 1) provide notification; or 2) obtain permission before disclosing any potentially relevant information. For example:

> Employee will obtain Company's written approval before publishing or submitting for publication any material (written, verbal, or otherwise) that relates to Employee's work at Company and/or incorporates any Proprietary Information.

At the same time, you want to encourage your employees to speak favorably to the press and while at speaking engagements without fear of being fired. Therefore, a clause incorporating some of the points below may be warranted.

> Notwithstanding the foregoing, it is understood that, at all such times, Employee is free to use information that is generally known in the trade or industry of Company, which is not gained as result of a breach of this Agreement, and Employee's own skill, knowledge, know-how, and experience to whatever extent and in whatever way Employee may wish.

Internal Disclosures

Merely preventing external disclosures is not enough. You need to ensure that ideas, expressions, concepts, designs, and other forms of innovation are brought to the forefront. If you don't know of an idea, how can you determine how to best protect it? Thus, it's often advisable to request employees to promptly disclose innovations as soon as possible. Further, consider whether your agreement should include sample invention disclosure forms. Whether such forms are mandated, consider at least requesting an explanation of:

- The novelty or distinctness of the invention or expression;
- How it differs from earlier or known inventions or expressions;
- Any tricks or parameters to best realize the benefits of the idea or expressions; and
- To provide drawings or sketches when feasible.

Aside from legal considerations, this allows other employees to replicate the invention or expression if the inventor ever leaves. More important, it drastically reduces the possibility that your application for rights (that is, a patent application) is not denied for insufficient information. For example, the patent laws of the United States require that the sought-after rights concern something that is new, novel, and nonobvious. Your patent application must also describe the invention in sufficient detail that a person skilled in the relevant art can make and use the claimed invention without undo experimentation. Additional laws require that the application identify the "best mode" for realizing the invention. Thus, not getting enough information about making and using the invention at the time the invention is created and perfected is a serious risk.

There is another reason to require inventors to promptly disclose this information. The gaming industry is a fast-paced industry. A lot of competitors may be innovating ideas that are similar, if not substantially similar, to the ideas for which you are—and they too likely are—filing patent applications. As a real-world example, I drafted and submitted a software-related application to the USPTO on behalf of a client. The USPTO rejected the application on a competitor's application that was filed a mere three weeks before our application. Luckily, the client had disclosure forms and correspondence from the inventors that clearly demonstrated that they invented the concept first and diligently worked to file the patent application. Thus, requesting that employees keep and maintain adequate and current records (in the form of notes, sketches, drawings, and in any other form) is advisable. Of course, the agreement should further indicate that such information is the company's property.

The Employee's Own IP

Returning to the issue of the employees' qualities that made your employees attractive, those qualities likely produced past successes, such as in the form of inventions and trade secrets that they themselves may own or otherwise be privy to. Thus, it's not only their past employers that you need to worry about. To further prevent any later allegations from the employee that you stole his or her personal inventions or ideas, many employment agreements also request that the employee list any prior inventions, including those obtained as a result of prior employment. Therefore, depending on their role, consider whether employees must list any such inventions, improvements, and so on that were owned or controlled by the employee prior to employment by your company.

While these provisions may effectively reduce the likelihood that your company will be tangled in a trade secret dispute, they may be incompatible. Specifically, you are asking for an employee to divulge prior inventions, which may inherently involve their and/or others' trade secrets or confidential information. Thus, consider reciting language that expressly acknowledges that you do not wish to receive such information, such as:

> Employee understands that if disclosure of any such Prior Invention pursuant to Section XX would cause him/her to violate any prior confidentiality agreement, Employee fully understands that he/she is not to list such Prior Inventions but only to disclose a cursory name for each Prior Invention, a listing of the party(ies) to whom it belongs, and the fact that full disclosure as to such Prior Invention has not been made for that reason. If no such disclosure is attached, Employee represents that there are no Prior Inventions.

» TESTING AGREEMENTS

Your game or hardware will likely undergo some beta-testing. Using a nondisclosure agreement will allow you to protect valuable trade secrets and dictate dissemination of other proprietary information. However, spend a bit of time thinking of your goals before determining how to conduct the testing and thus, what you expect from a nondisclosure agreement.

Specifically, you may want to use this opportunity to get more exposure such as from a trade journal or gaming blog. You may prefer that your beta-testers actually describe their experience. Ask yourself at least the following:

- What information must stay confidential?
- What information would you prefer to stay confidential but could live with its being made public if enough benefit stems from its disclosure?
- Can the testers disclose any information relating to their experience? And if so:
  - Do you have the opportunity to review it before public disclosure?
  - Is it limited to written or oral disclosure?

Spending a few minutes thinking about how the beta-testing can improve your position while ensuring that you protect your intellectual property rights will save a lot of time and frustration later in the process. In many circumstances, it's worth encouraging testers to write blogs or articles informing their readers of their experiences. Obviously, you want to ensure that regardless of what they write about, the bloggers or writers do not violate the confidentiality provisions of the agreement. Aside from legal issues, you want to keep these bloggers and writers happy—in the gaming world that means being one of the first to break the news of the latest and greatest product. Thus, in this field, long and tedious time restraints or requiring long periods for your receiving confirmation that their proposed articles don't contain confidential information will likely frustrate them. In this regard, the old way of doing things no longer applies. For example, agreements historically provided a snail mail address for communications relating to the contract. Provide an e-mail address and monitor it. It's often easier and keeps testers, consultants, or whomever happier with an easier way to communicate. Here is an example of language that you may want to consider:

> [DEVELOPER] understands that [TESTER] may wish to convey and/or publish opinions and impressions of [TESTER'S] experience with testing and/or analyzing [DEVELOPER's] systems and methods in connection with the Purpose, such as and including, periodicals, blogs, newsletters. [DEVELOPER] encourages [TESTER] to do so provided that no breach of the confidentiality provisions herein is made. If Recipient is unsure whether any publication or conveyance would breach any of the confidentiality provisions herein, Recipient is invited to transmit an electronic message to [developer@internetdomain] with the subject line of "Proposed Publication" with the proposed text to be conveyed or published. If [DEVELOPER] does not object or fails to object within 24 hours to the proposed text, then publication of the text will be deemed not a violation of the confidentiality provisions herein.

» CONTRIBUTION AGREEMENTS

You or your employees may be invited to speak at a seminar about the upcoming release of *Snowdown* or submit an article for a blog or journal about a new character for *Snowdown II*. Alternatively, you may have guest bloggers on your site. Who owns the copyright on the article or on any prepared materials? Can the speaker be recorded on electronic media? Who owns the recording? What if the submitted work shows great promise but doesn't quite fit your need? Can you edit it or will you allow someone else to edit your work? Is there a guarantee that you must publish any submitted work? These questions highlight some of the issues to consider before committing to speak or otherwise submit information. Either way, consider utilizing a simple contribution agreement to at least set forth who has what rights in certain copyrights. One example of a basic contribution agreement may include the following:

> Author hereby grants permission and license to Publisher to publish the article in print and/or electronic form ("Publication"), including the Internet, and the Publisher may at its discretion authorize reprinting and reuse of the article, with pledge to acknowledge the Author's authorship. Author acknowledges that submission of the Contribution is not a guarantee of publication. Author agrees not to republish the Contribution for at least one (1) year from the date of submission to Publisher. Author agrees that Publisher, its editors, contractors, and agents may edit the article for any purpose, including but not limited to style, length, content, consistency, and/or to provide editorial clarification.

> Author warrants that the Contribution is an original work by the Author, does not contain libelous or unlawful statements or medical claims, does not infringe upon the rights of others, contains no information that may cause harm or injury, and that the Author has the authority to grant the rights herein. Author agrees to indemnify and hold harmless the Publisher, its editors, contractors, and agents from any and all claims, damages, and expenses that may arise for alleged breach of Author warranties.

> Author retains all copyright rights in the Contribution except as provided herein. Publisher shall own and retain all other copyright rights in any and all Publications in which the Contribution is published (e.g., as a compilation).

Again, your primary focus may be protecting your company while encouraging bloggers and reporters to work with you in the future.

» ASSIGNMENTS

Throughout this chapter, we have discussed agreements in which an individual (such as a software engineer) or an entity (such as a production company) agrees to "assign" or "transfer" certain IP rights. For the most part, assignments are often utilized to transfer all rights, title, and interest, whereas licenses (discussed in Chapter 5) generally refer to agreements that grant a subset of rights. Do not, however, rely on these generic designations as a defining rule. Some licenses may convey essentially all rights, title, and interest while various assignments may convey only a portion of the available rights. Therefore, although the following discussion refers to transferring rights via an assignment, it should be understood that, in many cases, transfer of similar rights could be accomplished through licensing agreements, and vice versa.

What Rights?

Agreements in the video game industry often assign and/or license partial rights to a multitude of entities. In fact, your company may obtain the highest level of profit and diverse customer base by assigning or licensing rights in a piecemeal fashion to different entities. For example, you may assign patent rights relating to *Snowdown* between two competing companies—the first company may own the patent rights to certain technology in the United States for the Microsoft® Xbox 360 console, while another company owns the applicable patent rights to that technology only for use with another console, such as the Sony® PlayStation 3. Thus, you will want an assignment that assigns only a subset of the total rights to the relevant intellectual property. Rights can be split in a variety of ways, including:

- Geography (U.S. territory);
- Time (1 year);
- Product or platform (Xbox 360, PS3); or
- Many other distinctions that can be articulated.

Before going further, it's important to remember that each form of intellectual property is different and therefore there are important distinctions between assigning various forms of intellectual property. For example, when assigning (or being assigned) a partial percentage of the rights to a patent, it is important to note that each owner of a patent has an *equal right* to license or use the technology absent an agreement to the contrary. Therefore, even if you assign another party only 1 percent of a patent, that party can still exploit the patent to the same extent as an entity that has rights to the remaining 99 percent. This includes the possibility of granting a license to your competitor without first seeking your permission. Even worse, the individual or entity that has the 1 percent interest does not need to share any revenue generated from such use or licensing of the patented technology with you or any other co-owners.

Copyright ownership is a bit different. Similar to co-owners of a U.S. patent, co-owners of a copyrighted work have equal rights to use or transfer their rights to others independent of the other co-owners and to sue for infringement. However, unlike joint patent owners, joint copyright owners must provide their other co-owners with an accounting of the profits (that is, an equitable distribution of profits to other co-owners based on amount of work, investment, time, etc., to commercialize or exploit the work). Transfers of co-owned, divided copyright interests become complicated and in some instances might not be valid; this is yet another situation to be aware of and on which to consult an attorney on the ramifications of a potential assignment. In this regard, it's best to register a copyright with the U.S. Copyright Office before assigning any related rights. Registration is inexpensive and easy, as discussed in Chapter 1. The assignment of trademarks is generally similar with the caveat that any assignment of a trademark must also assign the goodwill associated with the mark.

Trade secrets are a bit different. Unlike other forms of intellectual property, trade secrets are governed by state law. Although most states have now adopted aspects of a uniform code, each state has its nuances. One issue to consider is how best to ensure the trade secret is properly assigned. For example, if you execute an agreement that assigns the right to *Snowdown* to another entity but you retain records and data relating to that trade secret, have you really assigned that right? Further, if you seek assignment of a trade secret, it's best to expressly recite that the rights also include the right to enforce any misappropriation of the trade secret.

Other issues that you may wish to address in an assignment include identifying which party is responsible for the prosecution of applications (patents or trademarks), such as the responsibility for filing papers with the USPTO; making prosecution decisions such as whether to file related applications (continuations and divisional or foreign applications); paying prosecution and maintenance fees and costs; paying litigation costs; and making litigation decisions.

You may want to consider whether to include reversion rights if an assignee doesn't meet certain terms as required by the assignment. Sublicensing issues may become important too. In this regard, unless prevented by the assignment, an assignee may sublicense to a related company or a competitor, allowing them to reap the majority of the profit from the technology. Incorporating restrictions or penalties for licensing or sublicensing may avoid some issues.

Timing Is Everything

Your focus and goals will vary significantly depending on whether you will be the assignor or the assignee and what the ultimate purpose of the assignment is. Even as an assignee, assignments are executed for various purposes. In some instances, you may be receiving patent rights via an assignment to obtain the rights to technology from another party; in other instances, you may be obtaining rights from your employees who invented the intellectual property you are trying to protect.

When is the best time to prepare the assignment? Obviously, there is no perfect answer, but it comes down to what is being assigned. For employee-based assignments, base them on a triggering event. For example, the above-referenced employment agreement may create an obligation for a software engineer to assign all its rights relating to *Snowdown*. For various reasons, however, it's best not to rely on the employee agreement alone. When, however, should the engineer assign the rights, such as to patentable subject matter?

At first glance, it may seem logical to immediately assign rights when submitting the idea for consideration. That obviously is ideal from the standpoint of reducing the risk that the engineer will leave the company before assigning the rights to your company. You may determine this is the best time for your company. There are, however, other considerations. Presume that the idea contains a lot of patentable subject matter. Patents empower the assignee with an exclusionary right to prevent others from making, using, selling, or importing the "claimed invention." Indeed, it is the claims of the patent that define the scope of your protection. Further, because claims define the invention, they determine who the proper inventor is. Therefore, by knowing the claims scope, you can more accurately determine which engineers, designers, and/or third parties contributed to the "invention," and who thus need to sign the assignment. Further, by signing the assignment after the claims have been drafted, there is no question that the inventors, in fact, have assigned the sought-after "invention." Further, because the patent application has been drafted, the assignments will assign the full subject matter of the submitted application. Therefore, for many circumstances, obtaining an assignment upon completion of the final draft of the patent application and submitting the assignment with the application or, alternatively, submitting the assignment immediately upon receiving an application number from the USPTO, is the best practice.

Going, Going, Gone

As discussed above, unforeseen circumstances may complicate completing the assignment agreement. Inventors may die, become incapacitated, or leave the company. Although a former engineer may be contractually bound to assign IP rights to *Snowdown*, the former employee may have moved, simply be uncooperative, or argue that the subject matter of the patent application for which you are seeking assignment includes information that does not fall under the obligations in the employment agreement (or any other relevant agreement). With the employment agreement in hand, there are processes for straightening out many issues, but why spend the money, time, and stress working out the issues after the fact? It's not worth delaying the release of *Snowdown* to ensure these issues are worked out. Even worse, imagine seeing an otherwise glowing review of *Snowdown* end with a sentence indicating that your company is currently engaged in a legal tiff with an old employee over rights to the game. Therefore, even if the assignment is eventually obtained, the headaches and effort involved may be minimized if you obtain the assignments sooner rather than later.

Filing, Filing, Filed

Clients often ask whether patent assignments must be filed at the Patent Office to be effective. This is referred to as "recording" an assignment. In short, we can't force you to do anything, but in view of the fact that the governmental fee is currently only $40, there are very few reasons, if any, not to file assignments. From a business perspective, potential investors need assurance that you actually own the rights. Nobody wants to gamble the farm for a $40 savings.

Legally, recording assignments with the Patent Office provides some very important benefits, specifically with regard to notice, and not recording assignments can have a potentially devastating effect. Recording provides "constructive notice" to all other potential purchasers, such as competitive development studios, of some or all rights relating to the patent. Constructive notice basically means that all potential purchasers of rights to that property are responsible for reviewing those records and cannot later argue that they were unaware of the transfer of property rights identified in a recorded document. Therefore, if you record an assignment in the Patent Office in accordance with the guidelines, if another party later obtains an assignment to those rights, you will not lose your assigned rights, even if that second purchaser honestly did not know about your assignment.

On the other hand, according to 35 U.S.C. § 261 (one of the sections of the U.S. patent laws), in some circumstances a previous assignment of a patent can actually be void against a second subsequent assignment of the same patent, unless the original assignment is recorded in the United States Patent and Trademark Office within 3 months of the date of execution or otherwise prior to the second subsequent assignment. That's a lot of security for a governmental fee of $40.

Let's presume that you want to save the $40 and don't file the assignment to a patent relating to Snowdown. An inventor leaves your company and, in exchange for compensation from your competitor, again assigns the same (or overlapping) rights to your competitor. If your competitor, without notice of the first assignment, records the second assignment before you do, you would need to sue the old employee who fraudulently transferred those rights to your competitor and prove in court that the former employee assigned his or her rights to you first. Compounding the issue is that the first assignment itself may be void under on 35 U.S.C. § 261. Needless to say, the odds are against you ever recouping the damage that employee caused, and the whole situation could have been avoided by recording the assignment for $40.

Make sure you identify your assignment properly. Because you are likely filing the assignment along with the application, you will not yet have the Patent Office's assigned application number. Thus, it's very important to ensure your assignment adequately identifies the submitted application. This can be done by using the application's title along with a unique identifier, such as an attorney docket number. When submitting an assignment for a patent application that has already been filed with the Patent Office, you must include the application number assigned by the Patent Office.

There are three elements that you *must* include on an assignment that does not have an application number: the date of execution, the names of each inventor and the title of the invention. Clearly, the names of the parties, an identification of the rights being transferred and a signature and date of execution of the inventors are all very important. Having a witness for the signatures may simplify proving that an inventor signed the document in case issues of proof arise later. Further, clauses requiring the inventors to cooperate in protecting the assigned rights and granting your attorneys the right to insert information, such as the application number, when received are very useful.

An assignment can include the assignment of "improvements," foreign rights, or future inventions. This may include continuation applications, continuation-in-part applications, divisional applications, and foreign filings. If assignments include "improvements," it is helpful to understand and define what is meant by improvements. Although later continuation and divisional applications inherit the assignment from a parent patent, the later applications will not have the assignment transferred to the record. Therefore, you may want to file a notice of recordation so that the Patent Office records for the later patents contain an indication of the assignment. More importantly, continuation-in-part applications and related applications that do not claim priority to the prior patent do not inherit an assignment from the prior patent. Therefore, a new assignment must be filed with the Patent Office in those cases.

IP Reward Programs

Using reward programs to compensate inventors for new ideas, inventions, and/or creative expression (read: graphics and artwork) may encourage prompt disclosure and encourage innovation. It can also, however, become expensive and require an abundance of administrative overhead. Using patents as an example, here are some (of the many) considerations for various implementations of a program to reward inventors. They may be used as initial thinking points when drafting your employment agreements or any other agreements that might affect patentable inventions.

One approach is to award inventors based only on the ideas that are ultimately filed in a patent application. This may provide a cost-effective approach because the company does not have to compensate employees for each and every idea that someone comes up with, but instead rewards the employee only for those ideas that the company deems worth pursuing in a patent application. Unfortunately, however, there are some drawbacks. First, upon implementation, you may notice an immediate spike in the average number of inventors listed for each patent application. This is a serious issue because incorrect inventorship, in extreme circumstances, can render your patent unenforceable. One client who rewarded its developers under this approach placed a cap on the total amount of compensation for each patent application such that after five inventors, each inventor would have to take a smaller cut. Needless to say, the number of inventors rarely exceeded five individuals after that.

Another issue you should address is that your intellectual property strategy may inadvertently, and possi-

bly adversely, impact some extremely valuable and bright
developers or other employees. Imagine an employee who is
a bright developer who submitted five invention disclosures—each of which was an excellent idea. In fact, the
ideas were so great, the company decided to retain them as
trade secrets instead of pursuing patent applications. In
this case, the bright developer is not rewarded for submitting any of the invention disclosures. This can lead
to a perception of unfairness, despite the fact that the
employee's ideas were off the chart. Imagine the difficulty
in informing the bright developer that his idea was patentable, however, for strategic reasons, the company decided
not to file for patent protection, and therefore, he will
not be compensated. Obviously, you can implement a system
where the value of the trade secret can be measured, but
if you do, ensure that too much time isn't wasted on determining and valuing the compensation to each employee. Also
be careful to value inventions consistently to avoid being
accused of favoritism.

Another approach may include rewarding inventors based
on the grant of a patent. This system more closely bases
the rewards on the company's benefit and may provide a more
accurate measure of compensation. Unfortunately, obtaining a patent in the software fields can take five or more
years, and sometimes employees are no longer with a company
by the time a patent is granted. Needless to say, this does
not provide an immediate reward and may be perceived as too
distant, but can also act as an incentive for an employee
to stay with a company, assuming that continued employment
is a condition of the reward.

Although there is no perfect system, you may discover
that the best-suited system for your purposes may be a combination of one or more of these approaches. Some companies
merge the two approaches and provide a nominal award when a
patent application is filed, and a more significant award
when the patent issues. The reward based upon issuance of
the patent is usually provided only if the inventor remains
employed by the company. Therefore, this mechanism may also
double as an employee retention mechanism, as indicated
above.

It goes without saying that no system is perfect. There
will always be at least one inventor who feels undercompen-
sated under any approach. Further, an overly complex reward
system can be an administrative burden, and may take valuable time away from harvesting and protecting the actual
ideas themselves. Therefore, you may discover that more
traditional compensation systems are more reliable. Regardless of what system is adopted, it never hurts to revisit
the issue every few years to consider how it may be improved
based on the changing needs and goals of the company.

» FINAL WORD

I hope this chapter has provided valuable insight into some of the issues you will encounter prior to, during, and following the development of your video game and other media-related inventions and ideas. The discussions were geared toward avoiding several of the pitfalls commonly encountered by developers. You will undoubtedly face additional issues; however, applying many of the concepts discussed above will serve as the groundwork and frame of reference to tackle those issues. In this regard, merely understanding the large and diverse role agreements often play in the development of video games and other media is truly the largest obstacle to overcoming the various issues. During a discussion with a developer regarding a specific IP agreement, he indicated that he did not realize that this specific agreement could have such wide-reaching implications for other forms of IP and the future of his invention. I ended my explanation with the sentence from G.I. Joe's public service announcements: "Now you know, and knowing is half the battle." Although we both got a laugh out of it, there is a lot of truth to it. I hope that half the battle is now over and you are more prepared to anticipate roadblocks before they arrive. With the proper understanding, roadblocks with dire consequences may also serve as opportunities to properly position your inventions and ideas.

CHAPTER **5**

LICENSING AND OPEN SOURCE MATERIAL

By Benjamin J. Siders

Most video games incorporate intellectual property belonging to a third party. This property could be the underlying game engine, artwork, sound recordings, or even dance choreography.[1] The Unreal II engine in particular was licensed for more than a dozen titles and the flexible Gamebryo engine runs everything from turn-based and real-time strategy games to massively multiplayer online role-playing games (MMORPGs) and action/adventure platform games.[2] Most products incorporate copyrighted artwork and audio produced and controlled by third parties, and the developer must beware of implicating competitive commercial rights such as trademarks, trade secrets, and rights of publicity. There are

---

1. *World of Warcraft* incorporates a number of humorous dance routines, such as the Macarena, Riverdance, Michael Jackson moves, and even Chris Farley's "Chippendales" routine from *Saturday Night Live*.

2. Gamebryo runs, among others, *Civilization IV, Zoo Tycoon 2, Prince of Persia 3D,* and *Warhammer Online*.

even risks in using apparently safe alternatives such as open source products. In short, *here be dragons.*

Obtaining the rights to use these properties usually means executing a licensing agreement with the rights holder, though alternatives exist and sometimes may be preferable. An entire book could be written (and many have been) about the intricacies of licensing intellectual property and we cannot hope to exhaustively cover the topic here. Rather, our purpose is to provide an overview of some of the special licensing concerns that attend their use. Like most conflicts, intellectual property disputes are more easily (and cheaply) disposed of when dealt with in advance.

This chapter will begin by examining general considerations applicable to licensing any kind of intellectual property as well as issues specific to certain types of property. Next, we will consider alternatives to the licensing model and the use of open source software. Finally, we will conclude with issues such as user-generated content, customization and modification, and First Amendment implications.

» FIVE QUESTIONS TO ASK YOUR LAWYER

You *do* have a lawyer, right?

While researching this chapter, I spoke with a game developer, who offered the following confession:

> The tendency of computer geeks to be know-it-alls extends to the legal arena as well. They tend to overestimate their legal knowledge and so they just "wing it" and write or amend their own contracts.

Would you trust a network API written by a lawyer? Then don't trust a contract written by a programmer. *Get a lawyer.*

Whether we call them licenses, agreements, waivers, releases, assignments, sales, covenants, promises, or guarantees, we are talking about contracts and contract law will govern the interpretation and enforcement of the license. Although portions of the entertainment industry operate in part through verbal contracts, the more common (and sensible) practice in the software industry is to draft and execute written licensing agreements that memorialize the parties' mutual understanding of their bargain. Reduced to its core, a license is a grant of permission by the intellectual property owner for somebody else (that is, you) to use the intellectual property. Licenses can be narrow and limited ("You may use a single, specific 30-second loop from my sound recording only on the main menu screen of one specific product.") or broad and wide-ranging ("You may make use of any song in our vast catalog of artists on any of your products for the next 10 years").

These are questions you should ask no matter what kind of IP you are licensing, and no matter what the particular needs of your product or business may be. We shall examine the terms that apply directly to your business needs in the section that follows these five questions.

1. Do You Even Need Permission?

Not all published information is protected intellectual property. You needn't acquire anybody's permission to use the text, story, or characters from *The Odyssey* in your game because that work is in the public domain.[3] Certain forms of expression are not copyrightable at all, such as raw data.[4] Conversely, works that we might intuitively guess to be in the public domain are actually copyrighted, such as "Happy Birthday to You."[5] Certain uses, even if commercial, might be considered fair uses and require no license. These inquiries require legal expertise in intellectual property law and your attorney is your best resource for this analysis. Every developer should have IP counsel on speed dial.

2. What Kind of Permission Do You Need?

A developer making a 3D murder mystery game bought a print of Dali's *The Temptation of Saint Anthony* at retail, digitized it, and hung a virtual copy on a virtual room in the game's virtual world, arguing that "I paid for it, and can do what I want with it. First-sale doctrine."

Not so.[6]

The sale of a *copy* is not the same as the sale of the *intellectual property rights*. The transfer of the intellectual property rights to a work from one person to another is commonly called an *assignment* and can be adequately conceptualized as "selling your rights." An assignment is different from a *license*. A license is a grant of permission ("you may come into my house") but an assignment is an absolute transfer of title ("you may *have* my house"). Sometimes, an assignment may be a more appropriate arrangement than a license.

For example, you may wish to hire a graphic artist to develop a company logo. You don't want a graphic artist claiming a copyright interest in your company logo after you've invested capital in building a brand around it. Similarly, you may hire freelancers on a one-off basis to produce graphic art and sound effects, some of which you may wish to alter and reuse. You may hire freelancers

---

3. However, other content contained in a publisher's version could be copyrightable and owned by the publisher (e.g., prefaces, annotations, and so forth).

4. However, the custodian of data can acquire proprietary or commercial rights in data under some circumstances, such as when the selection and arrangement of the data is original.

5. "Happy Birthday to You" will pass into the public domain in 2030, though its copyright status is frequently questioned.

6. The first-sale doctrine does grant the purchaser of a copy some limited discretion to redistribute that one copy regardless of whether the copyright owner has granted such permission. See 17 U.S.C. § 109(a).

to build a website, write the instruction manual, design box art, and so forth. An assignment of the rights to these works may be the preferred arrangement, and you may find yourself licensing the work back to the freelancer for the limited purpose of self-promotion in his or her portfolio.

3. What Laws Govern Your Transaction?

Whether an assignment or a license, the transaction will be covered in part by contract law, and in part by the body of law relating to the specific type of intellectual property you are transferring or licensing.

Contract interpretation is a matter of state law, but determining which state's contract rules govern the deal can itself become a complex (and expensive) inquiry. Imagine that the copyright holder is a Delaware corporation with headquarters in Seattle and your business is incorporated in New York but headquartered in Austin and you work in the San Diego office. The copyright holder signs the license from his Chicago studio and faxes it to the hotel business center in Cancun, where you're on vacation, and you sign it during a layover in Memphis. A year later, when a controversy erupts and you have to sue the licensor, you have since relocated to Miami and the copyright holder now lives in Toronto. Which state's (or nation's!) laws govern this deal?

Sound ridiculous? These kinds of tangled fact patterns are the stuff of attorneys' nightmares, and you can invest a substantial amount of cash just to figure out where you have to litigate, and which state's laws will govern the controversy. If the licensor disagrees, you could exhaust your budget simply trying to resolve this one issue.

Or, you could include choice of law and venue clauses in the license. As alluded to earlier, controversies are more easily (and cheaply) resolved in advance. Most licenses include choice of law and venue clauses, but you can't arbitrarily pick any state's law to govern unless that state is somehow connected to the transaction. Your attorney is the proper resource to consult to determine what your options are. Further, license agreements are often drafted by the licensor, who will invariably select his or her own state in the choice of law and venue clauses.

Do not overlook these clauses. If you are in San Diego and the venue for a dispute is New York, you have some ugly choices to face. You can either navigate New York courts and litigate New York law with California attorneys, or roll the dice on a local firm in New York that doesn't know you or your products. Either way, you are at a disadvantage in the event of a dispute.

In addition to contract considerations, there are certain federal laws that apply universally, such as the Sherman Act, a federal antitrust statute. The purpose of antitrust law is to encourage robust marketplace competition by placing limitations on anticompetitive business practices. Though licensing practices rarely run afoul of this rule, recall that Microsoft went to bat with the federal government over its licensing practices and is now subject to heightened regulation and scrutiny. Granted, we all would gladly accept this "problem" in exchange for Microsoft's market share, but the cautionary tale should not be overlooked. The successful antitrust plaintiff can recover treble damages and attorney fees, which would not otherwise be available in a contract dispute.

4. What Happens If There Is a Dispute?

Most disputes are resolved between the parties but irreconcilable differences sometimes require a third party to intervene. As alluded to above, a venue provision in the contract can save you an enormous amount of time and money by resolving the question, "Where can we sue them?" ahead of time.

However, lawsuits are an endangered species on account of the proliferation of mediation and arbitration clauses in contracts. These provisions may require the parties to go through a mediation before they may file a lawsuit, or they may waive the right to have your day in court completely by mandating the use of an arbitration panel. Such waiver provisions can work for or against you and should not be accepted lightly. Intellectual property law is complex and evolving at a very rapid pace. Arbitration panels may consist of people who are not experts in the particular property at issue and you are unlikely to get a panel of people who are familiar with the video game industry. Think carefully before you allow your license to be interpreted by people who don't understand your industry. Further, arbitration panels are generally composed of local attorneys and the legal industry is a small pond. A clause that requires you to air your grievances before an arbitration panel in the licensor's city may put you at a serious disadvantage, as the panel members will be much more familiar with the licensor and his attorneys, whereas you may be perceived as an out-of-towner making trouble for a local employer.

Another clause to consider is an attorney fees clause. Ordinarily, you cannot recover your legal expenses from the other side, even if you emerge victorious, unless a statute (such as the antitrust law) or a contract term provides for it. Legal fees are always a consideration when a business has to decide whether to vindicate rights. Is there a business justification for spending $25,000 on legal fees if the other side is demanding an extra $2,000 per year in licensing fees? You can simplify this choice by including a license term that allows you to recover attorney fees should you be forced to litigate or arbitrate the contract. Similarly, be aware that even attorney fees clauses that appear fair may contain hidden traps. If the venue clause requires you to travel to them, do you get your travel costs back if you win, as well?

Also bear in mind the availability of injunctive relief. An injunction from a court can legally prevent you from using the property you have licensed, either temporarily during the litigation or on a longer-term basis. This could effectively put an end to your business, even if you win!

5. How Will It End?

We rarely sign contracts with the expectation that a lawsuit will erupt, and we tend to overlook the terms governing the termination or breach of the license. Even when licenses end without controversy, a controversy later may make it relevant. For example, if your product uses a licensed game engine that contains security flaws, and a virus exploits those flaws and causes damage, the injured users may sue you for products liability. Is the licensor insured? Does the license require you to defend the suit or tender it to the licensor? Are you indemnified if you lose?

The most expensive part of litigation is attorney fees. Skilled lawyers, particularly in complex areas like IP law, may command a premium. Even if the licensor wrongfully files suit and your attorney successfully fends him off, your reward is likely to be a significant legal fee. In American law, you ordinarily cannot collect fees from the other side, even if you win, unless a law or contract term says otherwise. Beware of boilerplate licenses with onerous and one-sided fee-shifting clauses that require you to pay the licensor's legal fees without requiring the licensor to pay yours.

As alluded to in the opening paragraph, beware also of indemnification or other responsibility-shifting clauses that may impose upon you an affirmative obligation to give notice or tender the defense to the licensor or his counsel of choice in the event a suit is filed. Should you be sued and violate this obligation, the licensor will likely claim you breached a precondition to indemnification and you're on the hook. Now you have two lawsuits to deal with! Similarly, beware of boilerplate warranty disclaimers.

Further, be cognizant of nonassignability clauses or other limits on alienation. If the license is nonassignable and your company is acquired, you won't be able to transfer your right to use the intellectual property to the new owners without acquiring permission from the licensor. If you are being acquired, it's likely by a larger entity with more cash, and if the licensor stands between you and getting bought out, he has placed himself in an advantageous position to demand more money from either you or the parent company, or he can frustrate the deal.

Licenses may also require you to return, destroy, or otherwise dispose of your copies of the licensed property upon termination of the contract. Be certain that you will have no further need of the property before you agree to such terms.

Bankruptcies are also a consideration, as the income stream from your royalty payments may become a part of the bankruptcy estate if the licensor goes broke. The intellectual property might be sold to a creditor to satisfy outstanding debt obligations, and you may find yourself dealing with a new party who is less cooperative, or who will refuse to honor informal agreements or modifications to the license that you have struck with the licensor over time.

Finally, recall that even if you do everything right and win a lawsuit and are entitled to damages, if the other person has no cash to pay, your judgment is worthless. Shift this risk to a third party by procuring the proper form of insurance.

» COMMON LICENSE TERMS

Now that you are done talking with your attorney (you did finally call an attorney, right?) about the above five questions and he or she has produced a draft license for you to review, you should be sure it addresses at least all the major license terms. There are many ways to do this. For one, you can simply search online for sample licenses and compare what your attorney wrote. What follows is a template of common terms found in licensing agreements. Note that your specific license could contain additional terms or omit some of these, depending on the type of property and particular needs of you and the licensor.

Parties

A license should always clearly identify the parties, particularly if there is the possibility of confusion between an individual and a partnership or sole proprietorship, or where the licensor is a corporate entity.

Dates and Times

When was the license signed, and what is the "effective date" of the license? When can you start using the licensed property and when are payments due? Monthly? Annually? The first of the month? When is a payment delinquent? Are there late fees or penalties for late payments? Is the license perpetual? If not, when does it expire? Do you have the right to renew on the same terms? Does the license automatically renew? When must you give notice of your intent to renew/cancel? If this is an exclusive license, does the exclusivity provision have a sunset clause? Do warranties expire? A complex license may tie some or all of these terms back to the commencement date, or "effective date."

Recitals

This section of the license is full of sentences beginning with the word "whereas." The recitals set forth the factual background of the parties as they enter into the licensing agreement. These terms are useful if there is any confusion or uncertainty about the license and a judge, attorney, or mediator needs information about the circumstances surrounding the execution of the license. Recitals are not ordinarily binding, substantive terms that define each party's rights and responsibilities, but you should read them carefully to be sure they capture the facts accurately and beware of substantive license terms that incorporate or reference the recitals.

Definitions

Most nontrivial contracts have a section of definitions that are meant to improve readability. As a practical matter, the definitions section may not always be drafted with the substantive sections in mind, and vice versa, leading to confusion and uncertainty when the license is interpreted. Another pitfall is recursive definitions (for example, "Game Engine" is defined in part as "Software," and "Software" is defined in part as "Source Code" and "Source Code" is defined as the instruction set to the "Game Engine").

Grant of Permission

This section sets forth the actual rights you are acquiring to use the property, or what you're allowed to do with it. Consider the following grant of permission:

> Licensor hereby grants to Licensee a nonexclusive license to use any one (1) Sound Recording listed in the 2004 catalog of Licensor's Sound Recording Library in one (1) Product published by Licensee, such Product to be Published within two (2) years from the Effective Date of this License Agreement.

This appears straightforward enough, but what happens if you sign this agreement on January 1, 2006, incorporate a sound recording, complete the product, but for reasons beyond your control, the product cannot be published until 2009? Do you still have permission to use the sound recording? Does this license allow you to use any one sound recording as often as you like within the product or just once? Do you have permission to modify the recording? How is "product" defined? Can you use the sound recording in an expansion pack, or is that a separate "product"? What if the expansion pack is published more than two years later—is a separate agreement needed? Is the website for the game a separate "product"? Even a brief and straightforward grant of permission that appears clear and unambiguous can cause problems later.

For specific issues related to particular types of property, such as "personal" licenses and reservations of rights, see the section titled Specific Properties, below.

Payment

Sometimes called "consideration," a legal term of art, or a "royalty," payment terms can be structured in any way the parties like. You might pay a monthly or annual fee to use any property in the licensor's music catalog (that is, licensing broadcast rights from ASCAP), or you might pay a fee for every copy of your product sold. This fee could be fixed, or a function of sale price. One thing to bear in mind is that in ordinary contract principles, a gratuitous promise unsupported by consideration is *not enforceable*.

The payment terms can be extremely detailed ("Licensee shall transfer $50,000 in United States dollars on the 15th day of each month via wire transfer to Account No. 867-53-09 held at The Very Big Bank of America, 1 Wall Street, New York, NY") or simply set a price or means for calculating price and contain no other provisions. Beware also of minimum (and maximum) payment terms. These can be periodic minimums ("no less than $5,000 monthly") or a license lifetime minimum. Be alert for such terms, as you might be forced to make payments for property that you ultimately do not use, such as if the project is canceled. Also beware of lifetime minimums that could accrue into a large balloon payment due when the license terminates.

Note also that the tax treatment of cash payments may influence how you wish to negotiate the payment schedule.

Other Terms

As discussed in the earlier section titled Five Questions to Ask Your Lawyer, there are other standard terms you should expect to see that don't generally relate to your specific business needs such as choice of law, venue, indemnification, termination, warranties and disclaimers, attorney fees and cost shifting, severability and merger clauses, assignability, and so forth.

» SPECIFIC PROPERTIES

Copyrights

Copyrights are probably the most heavily licensed property in the gaming industry. Sound recordings, game engines, source code, artwork, instruction manuals, documentation, compilers, music: these things are all subject to copyright.

Copyrights are set forth in the Constitution as a means for promoting science and the "useful arts" and the Constitution allows the recognition of copyrights only for a limited time. Copyrights are also exclusively the domain of Congress, and thus of federal law. That is, there is generally no state law of copyrights, though nonprotected items not covered by the Copyright Act may be protected by state copyright laws.

Copyrights are somewhat unique among the various intellectual properties in that different pieces of the copyright rights may be licensed on different terms to different people, or relicensed to multiple people.

The Copyright Act sets forth the panoply of exclusive rights an author of a work protected by the Act receives. These are the right to reproduce, prepare derivative works, distribute copies, perform the work, and display the work publicly. Also note that the duration of copyright rights is limited by the Constitution. Though these durations are extremely long, once the copyright expires the work becomes public domain and may be used without anybody's permission indefinitely. Don't sign a contract in which you agree to pay royalties beyond the copyright duration!

The copyright rights can also be handed out individually, and vague grants of permission don't always convey enough information. Which of these exclusive rights is included in a license to "use" a sound recording in your product? Do you need a right to "display" artwork publicly if you're licensing artwork for your public website? What about a private site only for your subscribers? Or for your development team? When somebody connects to your browser, they will download a copy. Do you have a license to distribute copies? You should hammer out the exact use you intend to make of the product, and be sure you have acquired the proper permissions.

Perhaps because of these pitfalls and complications, developers often prefer to simply "buy" a copyright by hiring freelancers to produce a work for hire, which vests the copyrights in the developer rather than the author. However, you may find yourself the *licensor* in this situation, as freelancers often wish to obtain permission to use the work for self-promotion in their portfolios. While this is innocent on the surface, consider the likelihood that a freelancer's future client will point to an item in the portfolio and say, "Make me something that looks like that."

If the freelancer simply copies what he or she produced for you and modifies it for the next client, has he or she produced a derivative copy in violation of *your* rights? You may not care until the freelancer is selling derivatives of your entire user interface to a developer who is producing a clone of your product to compete with you in the marketplace.

Trademarks

Trademarks exist in both state and federal law and are recognized and governed primarily by the Lanham Act. Unlike patents and copyrights, on which the Constitution imposes limited durations, trademark rights can last indefinitely.

Trademarks may be both licensed and assigned, but if the assignment of the trademark does not include the goodwill associated with the mark, the assignment is known as a "naked assignment" and passes no rights. For an idea of how trademark licensing works, consider McDonald's. Individual McDonald's restaurants are generally privately held small businesses owned by individuals who license the McDonald's trademarks. The license requires each McDonald's store to comply with the standards set by the larger McDonald's organization so that all stores are uniform in appearance, food quality and taste, and customer experience. Thus, whether you walk into a McDonald's in Iowa City, Oklahoma City, or New York City, you know what to expect. It is precisely this settled consumer expectation about the store that gives a McDonald's franchise its commercial value.

But imagine if McDonald's licensed its trademark without the accompanying standards, and each store owner could produce a different product and call it a "Big Mac" and could decorate the store in any way. Going to a McDonald's would be no different from going to any random restaurant, and the commercial identity of "McDonald's" would be lost. This is the essence of trademark licensing.

If you license trademark rights, you almost certainly will be held to some kind of "quality control" standards that will impose obligations and duties upon you to comply with certain standards, procedures, and a minimum level of quality as a condition of using the trademark. These duties can be expensive, requiring you to document processes, submit reports, allow random inspections, send product samples, and perform whatever other steps or procedures the trademark owner may wish to impose. You will generally perform these obligations at your own expense, on top of whatever fee you pay to use the mark itself.

Another consideration with trademarks is that they can cover more than the name of a business. The "look and feel" of a product can be distinctive enough to warrant trademark protection, as can the packaging. This is so-called "trade dress" infringement and before you simply copy another product wholesale, you must determine whether you need to license the trade dress.

In a real world example, a small developer wished to produce a Facebook game that was essentially an online version of a popular board game with some altered game mechanics to allow for an endless game experience. Imagine a game of Monopoly with limitless properties to purchase and means for tearing down an opponent's houses and hotels.[7] The project never got off the ground because the owner of the board game property refused to license it and the game developer didn't want to put the capital at risk to build it only to face an immediate lawsuit for trade dress infringement.[8]

While imitation may be the sincerest form of flattery, it can also be an easy way to unwittingly invite a lawsuit.

Rights of Publicity and Model Releases

While we don't ordinarily think of the right of publicity as having anything to do with gaming, consider whether recent events covered extensively on channels like E! may affect the business decisions of Electronic Arts regarding its Tiger Woods PGA Tour family of products, or whether Ben Roethlisberger will ever again grace the cover of EA's *Madden NFL* franchise.[9]

Despite the widespread celebrity worship phenomenon in the United States, the doctrines surrounding the right of publicity are not especially well-defined or well-understood. Publicity rights will be defined in state statute in some jurisdictions, and by common law in the rest. Most jurisdictions recognize the assignability of rights of publicity, but this is one area where the choice of law provision may be critically important to defining the scope of rights you receive (or can license at all).

Related to the right of publicity is the concept of "likeness" rights, which is the right to control the commercial use of one's personality. This may also seem generally irrelevant to gaming, but did that license you executed with Paramount to use the Indiana Jones property include the likeness of Harrison Ford? Does

---

7. For the record, the board game publisher was not Parker Brothers.

8. Even if the odds of such a lawsuit being successful are low, it must be taken seriously and few small businesses want to fund a legal defense team before the product is even out the door.

9. Both Woods and Roethlisberger were recently involved in personal issues that affected the public's perception and thus the marketability of their names and personas.

your license to use Tolkien's Middle Earth setting include the likeness of Viggo Mortensen, or must you re-imagine Aragorn? Will a different "look" for the character confuse your players, many of whom may know the character only from the films?

When considering publicity licenses, consider whether you are acquiring the right to use the person's name, likeness, personality, or some combination of these. Also consider the circumstances under which you may terminate the license (and thus stop paying), such as if the licensor's image suffers serious tarnishment.

Note also that there are some First Amendment limits to the right of publicity. For example, the names and images of celebrities are used daily in news reporting, and such use is protected by the First Amendment. Tiger Woods cannot stop an artist from producing an artist rendering of Woods' record-breaking victory at Augusta.[10]

If you plan on hiring independent actors or models for photography, motion capture, video, or voiceover, be sure to obtain a model release from each individual. A sample model release is included on the attached CD. Also, if you hire an actor who is a member of an actors' union, e.g., the Screen Actors Guild (SAG) or American Federation of Television and Radio Artists (AFTRA), there are a few extra hoops you will need to jump through. For example, if you want to hire a SAG actor, with limited exceptions, your company must be a signatory to the current SAG Interactive Media Agreement. For more information, see http://www.sag.org/newmedia (SAG: New Media) and http://www.aftra.org/contracts.htm (AFTRA: Interactive Media).

Trade Secrets

Trade secrets are a special form of intellectual property, roughly defined as a kind of information whose value is derived primarily from the fact that the information is not public. The simplest example is food recipes, which are essentially lists of instructions and therefore not copyrightable. However, companies invest substantial resources in keeping secret the seasoning recipes for major products, and the law recognizes these "trade secrets" as a form of protected intellectual property.

Trade secrets protect much more than food, however. They also protect know-how, ideas, and facts—things not ordinarily protected in law. Formulas, equations, mathematical processes, file formats, communications protocols—any secret information from which one can gain a competitive advance or economic advantage by maintaining its secrecy is potentially protected by trade secret law, and licensing terms are often strict and require certain procedures and controls to ensure that secrecy is maintained. Once a trade secret is public, it's no longer

10. ETW v. Jireh Pub. Inc., 332 F.3d 915 (6th Cir. 2003).

protected as a trade secret and anybody is free to use it without paying any licensing fees.

Well, *almost* anybody. If you've already signed a contract to pay licensing fees in exchange for using a trade secret, you may have to keep paying even if the trade secret is later revealed.[11] Indeed, you could be compelled to pay royalties indefinitely for use of a trade secret that has since become public knowledge, and can be utilized for free by later competitors, unless your contract contains contrary terms.

Patents

Like it or not, software is patentable subject matter. But what does this mean? As discussed in Chapter 1, if software is useful, new, and nonobvious, the developer can get a patent for it. But is all software patented? Do you need to license someone's patent every time you release software? No, and, well, maybe.

You might have developed your software from scratch, but someone else might own a patent that claims—i.e., protects—a similar feature. This is commonly known as innocent infringement, which, unfortunately, is no defense in patent litigation. If another company owns a patent, it might come after you and request that you pay it a license fee.

In addition, there are many nonpracticing entities (NPEs)—aka, patent trolls—that own valuable patents and that are not afraid to sue people for royalties. If you are found guilty of patent infringement, you face a court injunction to stop selling your product, thereby ending your income stream. If you are found guilty of *willful* patent infringement, a court has discretion to award up to *triple damages* to the patent holder! NPEs thus have a lot of leverage to get you to settle quickly for a handsome royalty so that you can keep selling your product and make money, regardless of whether you believe you actually infringe the patent or not.

What does this mean, though? Do you need to do a patent search every time you launch a new product? It depends. The rule today is that you must not act recklessly. More specifically, proof of willful infringement permitting enhanced damages requires at least a showing of *objective recklessness*, i.e., that the infringer acted despite an objectively high likelihood that its actions constituted infringement of a valid patent. If you are actually aware of a patent that you have reason to believe protects any aspect of your product, then you need to speak with a patent attorney. Remember, the goal here is to avoid litigation, regardless of whether you believe that you actually infringe any patents.

---

11. The classic example is the antiseptic mouthwash product Listerine. After the formula for Listerine was published, a licensee argued he shouldn't have to pay licensing fees for it any more. The courts disagreed. Warner-Lambert Pharm. Co. v. John J. Reynolds, Inc., 178 F.Supp. 655 (S.D.N.Y. 1959), aff'd 280 F.2d 197 (2d Cir. 1960).

Licensing Databases

There remains a category of information that is not protected by *any* form of intellectual property, but which some enterprise has invested significant capital to gather and compile. These are databases of information (often publicly available information) that are not protected under any legally recognized form of intellectual property. Examples include things such as telephone books, lead lists, marketing directories, property directories, site aggregators, and so forth.

Unless there is originality in the selection and/or arrangement of the data, the information contained in these databases is not protected by any intellectual property. However, a license may nevertheless be required to access the information. Somebody funded the effort to collect it, and somebody expects to be paid for it.

The important lesson here is that just because you *can* get information that is not protected by any intellectual property does not necessarily give you the right to do with it as you please. The law in this area continues to develop and emerge, but a few principles have been established firmly enough that you should contract around them. For example, price discrimination when licensing databases is an acceptable practice, and while you might be able to acquire data at a low price (possibly even free) for personal use, you likely violate the licensing terms when you incorporate the data into a commercial product.[12]

Likewise, websites may make data available to the public, with an implied or even explicit license on how that data may be used. For example, game developers may be interested in websites that publish random numbers sequences based on isotopic decay, for use in scientific studies and statistics. While this information may be free to scientists and academics, it's not necessarily freely licensed to a commercial enterprise. Similarly, so-called "screen scrapers" can automatically scan websites for news and competitors' prices or query databases to gradually extract their contents, and then compile this information. Such uses may violate terms of service that operate as an effective license, exposing you to liability.

The lesson here is that just because you can get to data does not necessarily make it freely available to you without cost. Be aware of the potential for implied or express licenses connected to "free" information that may implicate how and when you may use that information.

» ADVERTISING AND PRODUCT PLACEMENT

Leela: *Didn't you have ads in the 21st century?*

Fry: *Well sure, but not in our dreams. Only on TV and radio, and in magazines, and movies, and at ball games, and on buses and milk cartons and t-shirts, and bananas and written on the sky. But not in dreams. No siree!*[13]

---

12. ProCD, Inc. v. Ziedenberg, 86 F.3d 1447 (7th Cir. 1996).
13. Futurama, *A Fishful of Dollars* (Orig. air date April 27, 1999).

Product placement is everywhere, and while the adage "There's no such thing as bad press" may hold in the marketing industry, this is not a rule recognized in American law. Brand recognition and reputation is valuable and expensive to develop but trivial to destroy. Good custodians of branded properties aggressively police their use to ensure that their brands and products are not threatened through haphazard public use or unwanted associations with unpopular public figures.

This may seem an esoteric concern, but product placement trademark issues can sneak up upon the unwitting designer. For example, virtually every game involving car racing or sports requires the use of trademarked property. Even flight simulators and war games can implicate this concern. If you don't want a cease-and-desist letter from the multibillion dollar banking, chemical, automotive, and electronics holding company known as Mitsubishi Group, you might talk to your lawyer before you include that Mitsubishi Zero in your World War II game.

Further, companies may not want to be associated with your product, or—backward as it may seem—they may expect to be compensated for inclusion in your product. While it may seem counterintuitive that a company would expect to be paid for brand exposure, consider the racing example above. In a game where people compare the virtual performance of highly recognizable and popular automotive brand names, you can bet that the manufacturer will expect some compensation for the risk inherent in that kind of exposure.[14] Likewise, certain brands will sell themselves and can move an otherwise unremarkable product. Brands such as the NFL and its affiliated teams are some examples. These adroitly manicured brands are owned by companies that rigorously enforce their trademark rights to avoid blows to their brand reputation.

Further, including everyday products in your game world can land you in trouble. Including every day objects in your game can lend realism and polish to your game's look-and-feel, but always beware of the pitfalls of inadvertent product placement. Is that your villain holding an iPod while drinking from a bottle of Jack Daniels? Did you learn whether Corona has any trademark rights in the "lime-stuck-in-the-neck" gimmick? Is that green tractor going to attract the attention of John Deere's in-house counsel?[15] Did your artist use pink insulation in that murder scene that takes place inside an attic?[16]

It's worth noting that not every use of a brand or trademark is a violation of the brand's rights, but the point isn't whether you have the right, in the abstract, to use a mark. That's an academic question for law students. As a budding entrepreneur, the point is to avoid having to fund a legal battle over these issues in the first place. Even when drafting dialog scripts, one must always be cognizant that

---

14. For example, suppose an error in your physics engine causes the Corvette to drastically underperform or gives a sporty coupe a sluggish feel while handling. Could that implicate popular perceptions of the brand? Does your license agreement with the automaker insulate you from any liability for that kind of error?

15. Yes, John Deere owns a trademark in a specific shade of green as used on farming equipment.

16. *In re* Owens-Corning Fiberglas Corp., 774 F.2d 1116 (Fed. Cir. 1985).

names that we use casually in everyday speech may not be appropriate for inclusion in the game because they are trademarks. At one point, somebody owned the trademark rights to products like aspirin, escalator, zipper, and butterscotch. Now, companies fight hard to ensure that they don't lose their rights to brands like Rollerblade, Xerox, Kleenex, BAND-AID, and Corn Flakes. Sloppy usage of trademarks in your product can imply endorsement or simply weaken the mark by using it generically. Either use invites the unwanted attention of corporate counsel.

» OPEN SOURCE LICENSING

No discussion of third-party licensing would be complete without a discussion of the *open source* software movement. Much confusion attends this topic, but the key issue to note is that open source is not the same as *free*. That is, an open source product license does not necessarily grant to the world unfettered access to the code and software. Quite the opposite, open source software is sometimes strictly licensed, and onerous limitations can be imposed on your ability to reuse and redistribute your product in downstream commerce. Further, open source products sometimes make use of licenses written imprecisely and informally by a developer. Such licensed use often contains hopelessly vague language and abbreviated terms that fail to cover the issues discussed above.[17]

As mentioned, *open source* software is often confused with *free* software, but open source is free in the sense of the word that pertains to *liberty*, not *price*.[18] That is, the code may be freely used by whoever agrees to the open source licensing terms. However, this is not necessarily the same as not having to pay for it. While, as a rule, open source code does not have to be purchased, open source licenses frequently contain restrictions on the downstream use of products into which they are incorporated.

Here is an example of an informally written open source license created by college students in the 1990s to accompany their online role-playing game (RPG) product, once known as a *MUD*:

> **!! DikuMud is NOT Public Domain, shareware, careware or the like !!**
>
> You may under no circumstances make profit on **ANY** part of DikuMud in any possible way. You may under no circumstances charge money for distributing any part of dikumud [sic]—this includes the usual $5 charge for "sending the disk" or "just for

---

17. This practice has declined in favor of more standard open source licenses.
18. A common quip among open source developers is "Free as in speech, not free as in beer."

> the disk" etc. By breaking these rules you violate the agreement between us and the University, and hence will be sued.
>
> Any running version of DikuMud must include our names in the login sequence. Furthermore the "credits" command shall always cointain [sic] our name, addresses, and a notice which states we have created DikuMud.

Despite this apparent clarity, the authors did not use legal terminology such as *consideration*, but instead the more vague term *profit*, leading to much confusion among MUD developers as to whether, and how, they could engage in cost recovery while using a DikuMUD code base.

These are legitimate concerns even for major commercial projects. The popular MMORPG *EverQuest* was created by DikuMUD players and the game included wording identical to that found in the DikuMUD source code. This in turn led to a minor controversy that was put to rest only when the game's publisher, Verant, issued a sworn statement that the product was not built on the DikuMUD source code. Although the DikuMUD authors shrugged it off, it's not unthinkable that a more opportunistic author in DikuMUD's position may be inclined to saber-rattle in hopes of scoring a quick settlement at your expense.

The point of this section is not to discourage you from using open source products,[19] but only to help you understand that open source products are licensed and you should be cognizant of the licensing terms and their implications before you decide to incorporate the code into your project. If the terms are unworkable, heed the advice contained in the DikuMUD license:

> These are very generous terms for any software. If you don't want to accept them, feel free to run some other software, or write your own.

The *Open Source Initiative* maintains a comprehensive list of open source licenses at http://www.opensource.org/licenses/index.html.

» THE FIRST AMENDMENT

Although the United States enjoys very liberal and broad free speech rights, these rights are not entirely unfettered. Trademark and copyright owners often have rights that conflict with free speech rights, and free speech doesn't always prevail. For example, while you may *really* want to include recognizable brands in your game, the names of these products (and in some cases, their likenesses) are often

---

19. Indeed, the author is a former open source developer.

protected by trademarks, whose owners may not wish to be associated with your product[20] or may expect payment in exchange for the privilege.

Whether or not this practice runs afoul of your right to free expression, the point is to avoid an unnecessary and expensive legal battle that will drain your resources and distract you from the business of making video games. Sony was famously sued by a group of plaintiffs who claimed that Sony violated their trademark rights by digitally altering the billboards in Times Square for the movie *Spider-Man 2*. A federal district judge sharply dismissed the lawsuit on various grounds, including First Amendment protection, but Sony still had to pay counsel to fight it. Sony has the resources to underwrite this kind of lawsuit; do you? Is it worth a five- or six-digit legal bill to establish your right to use the term *iPod* in your product, or can you just make up a similar device for use in your product that won't invite the unwanted attention of Apple's attorneys?

The issue is also not confined to trademarks. How much of Edgar Allan Poe's "The Raven" can your character recite in dialog before you get into trouble?[21]

Although we enjoy broad First Amendment protection in our creative expression, those rights can bump up against the commercial rights of others, and when these others are mass media conglomerates with effectively bottomless pockets to aggressively pursue and protect their commercial interests in their intellectual property, being right on the law isn't enough. The old adage "How much justice can you afford?" comes into play. Your business is producing video games, not financing legal debates over the nuances of free expression.

---

20. Hypothetically, imagine if the protagonist in *Grand Theft Auto* was modeled in a Focus on the Family T-shirt. At a minimum, Rockstar could expect a very serious cease-and-desist letter from counsel.

21. Trick question. "The Raven" is now in the public domain.

CHAPTER **6**

WEB SITE LEGAL POLICIES

By C. Andy Mu, Rajit Kapur, and Ross Dannenberg

» INTRODUCTION

So you have just finished developing the next *World of Warcraft*® or *Halo*®. What now? Of course, you want to begin selling the game, recovering development expenses, and, hopefully, making a profit. But before you start setting up a road-side stand, signing up for the Apple® App Store, or calling video game outlets to stock your game, consider whether you have adequately protected your game from unauthorized uses including illegitimate copying and distribution. No? Don't worry, there are multiple ways in which a software developer may protect its interests while maintaining the commercial viability of its game.

This chapter offers a glimpse into commonly used legal policies and agreements for appropriately controlling the use and distribution of your game and avoiding potential liabilities. Specifically, this chapter offers an introduction to end-user license agreements (EULAs) and terms of use (TOU) agreements as two of the primary ways in which to control use and distribution. EULAs and TOU agreements are similar in many ways, particularly with respect to their intended purpose and objectives. Perhaps the chief distinction between the two is in their respective application: EULAs are generally used with purchased or downloaded software while TOU agreements are typically used with web-based games and other web-related content. Lastly, we also briefly address privacy policies and copyright policies. Privacy policies let users know how you intend to use information you gather about them. Copyright policies let users know how you address copyrighted content uploaded by users (if allowed) and also how you address alleged violations of the Digital Millennium Copyright Act (DMCA).

» EULAS

Typically, protecting your video game from copying, modification, and redistribution is established by the use of an end-user license agreement (EULA). EULAs define the allowable scope of a purchaser's ability to copy, modify, and/or distribute a copy of the software. EULAs operate under an established system in the software industry where a user purchases a license to the software, not a copy of the software. By licensing the use of the software instead of selling copies of the software itself, a company may control the use of the software based on the terms of the EULA. In many cases, the EULA is not known to the purchaser until the point of installation and, oftentimes, installation of the software is conditioned on acceptance of the EULA. Figure 1 illustrates a sample EULA (a copy of the sample EULA is included on the attached CD).

Figure 1 Sample End-User License Agreement (EULA)

END-USER LICENSE AGREEMENT FOR {INSERT PRODUCT NAME} IMPORTANT PLEASE READ THE TERMS AND CONDITIONS OF THIS LICENSE AGREEMENT CAREFULLY BEFORE CONTINUING WITH THIS PROGRAM INSTALL: {INSERT COMPANY NAME}'s End-User License Agreement ("EULA") is a legal agreement between you (either an individual or a single entity) and {INSERT COMPANY NAME} for the {INSERT COMPANY NAME} software product(s) identified above which may include associated software components, media, printed materials, and "online" or electronic documentation ("SOFTWARE PRODUCT"). By installing, copying, or otherwise using the SOFTWARE PRODUCT, you agree to be bound by the terms of this EULA. This license agreement represents the entire agreement concerning the program between you and {INSERT COMPANY NAME}, (referred to as "licenser"), and it supersedes any prior proposal, representation, or understanding between the parties. If you do not agree to the terms of this EULA, do not install or use the SOFTWARE PRODUCT.

The SOFTWARE PRODUCT is protected by copyright laws and international copyright treaties, as well as other intellectual property laws and treaties. The SOFTWARE PRODUCT is licensed, not sold.

1. GRANT OF LICENSE.
The SOFTWARE PRODUCT is licensed as follows:
(a) Installation and Use.
{INSERT COMPANY NAME} grants you the right to install and use copies of the SOFTWARE PRODUCT on your computer running a validly licensed copy of the operating system for which the SOFTWARE PRODUCT was designed [e.g., Windows 95, Windows NT, Windows 98, Windows 2000, Windows 2003, Windows XP, Windows ME, Windows Vista].
(b) Backup Copies.
You may also make copies of the SOFTWARE PRODUCT as may be necessary for backup and archival purposes.

2. DESCRIPTION OF OTHER RIGHTS AND LIMITATIONS.
(a) Maintenance of Copyright Notices.
You must not remove or alter any copyright notices on any and all copies of the SOFTWARE PRODUCT.
(b) Distribution.
You may not distribute registered copies of the SOFTWARE PRODUCT to third parties. Evaluation versions available for download from {INSERT COMPANY NAME}'s websites may be freely distributed.
(c) Prohibition on Reverse-Engineering, Decompilation, and Disassembly.
You may not reverse-engineer, decompile, or disassemble the SOFTWARE PRODUCT, except and only to the extent that such activity is expressly permitted by applicable law notwithstanding this limitation.
(d) Rental.
You may not rent, lease, or lend the SOFTWARE PRODUCT.
(e) Support Services.
{INSERT COMPANY NAME} may provide you with support services related to the SOFTWARE PRODUCT ("Support Services"). Any supplemental

software code provided to you as part of the Support Services shall be considered part of the SOFTWARE PRODUCT and subject to the terms and conditions of this EULA.

(f) Compliance with Applicable Laws.

You must comply with all applicable laws regarding use of the SOFTWARE PRODUCT.

3. TERMINATION

Without prejudice to any other rights, {INSERT COMPANY NAME} may terminate this EULA if you fail to comply with the terms and conditions of this EULA. In such event, you must destroy all copies of the SOFTWARE PRODUCT in your possession.

4. COPYRIGHT

All title, including but not limited to copyrights, in and to the SOFTWARE PRODUCT and any copies thereof are owned by {INSERT COMPANY NAME} or its suppliers. All title and intellectual property rights in and to the content which may be accessed through use of the SOFTWARE PRODUCT is the property of the respective content owner and may be protected by applicable copyright or other intellectual property laws and treaties. This EULA grants you no rights to use such content. All rights not expressly granted are reserved by {INSERT COMPANY NAME}.

5. NO WARRANTIES

{INSERT COMPANY NAME} expressly disclaims any warranty for the SOFTWARE PRODUCT. The SOFTWARE PRODUCT is provided "As Is" without any express or implied warranty of any kind, including but not limited to any warranties of merchantability, noninfringement, or fitness of a particular purpose. {INSERT COMPANY NAME} does not warrant or assume responsibility for the accuracy or completeness of any information, text, graphics, links, or other items contained within the SOFTWARE PRODUCT. {INSERT COMPANY NAME} makes no warranties respecting any harm that may be caused by the transmission of a computer virus, worm, time bomb, logic bomb, or other such computer program. {INSERT COMPANY NAME} further expressly disclaims any warranty or representation to Authorized Users or to any third party.

6. LIMITATION OF LIABILITY

In no event shall {INSERT COMPANY NAME} be liable for any damages (including, without limitation, lost profits, business interruption, or lost information) rising out of "Authorized Users" use of or inability to use the SOFT-

WARE PRODUCT, even if {INSERT COMPANY NAME} has been advised of the possibility of such damages. In no event will {INSERT COMPANY NAME} be liable for loss of data or for indirect, special, incidental, consequential (including lost profit), or other damages based in contract, tort, or otherwise. {INSERT COMPANY NAME} shall have no liability with respect to the content of the SOFTWARE PRODUCT or any part thereof, including but not limited to errors or omissions contained therein, libel, infringements of rights of publicity, privacy, trademark rights, business interruption, personal injury, loss of privacy, moral rights, or the disclosure of confidential information.

Source: http://www.developer-resource.com/sample-eula.htm.

As shown in Figure 1, a EULA will generally include a preamble or introduction followed by several clauses that govern different aspects of a purchaser's use and rights as well as the software developer's rights, warranties, and liabilities. Most EULAs begin with an explicit indication that the agreement is contractually binding and is required prior to authorized installation and use of the software. The introduction should also make a point of noting that the software is licensed, not sold, so that the relationship is clear to the end-user. A license versus a sale is an important distinction to note as a sale gives rise to end-user rights under the first-sale doctrine. In particular, under the first-sale doctrine, once a copyrighted work such as software is sold, the copyright owner no longer has control over the subsequent transfer of ownership of that specific copy of that work.[1] However, if the copy of the software is only licensed, the copyright holder is still entitled to control subsequent distribution or sale of that copy of the software.

For a EULA to be properly interpreted as a license, courts have generally looked to three factors: 1) whether the copyright owner specifies that a user is granted a license; 2) whether the copyright owner significantly restricts the user's ability to transfer the software; and 3) whether the copyright owner imposes notable use restrictions.[2] The template EULA shown in Figure 1, as will be described in further detail below, offers sample clauses, conditions, and limitations that a court will likely find adequate. For example, the Grant of License clause explicitly indicates that the user is granted a license, rather than a sale. The Distribution and Rental subclauses (b and d) of section 2, on the other hand, clearly indicate a restriction of the end-user's ability to transfer the software while the Prohibition on Reverse Engineering, Decompilation, and Disassembly subclause of section 2 provides one example of a restriction on use. Accordingly, you should confirm

---

1. *See* 17 U.S.C. § 109.
2. Vernor v. Autodesk, Inc., 621 F. 3d 1102, 1111 (Fed. Cir. 2010); *see also* United States. v. Wise, 550 F.2d 1180, 1190–1192 (9th Cir. 1977).

that such clauses (or versions of these clauses) have been sufficiently incorporated into your EULA.

With respect to scope of the license, EULAs generally include a clear and complete listing of all portions of the video game that are governed by the EULA including any online aspects (e.g., virtual worlds) and offline components that might not be required for a certain mode of game play (e.g., game clients needed for online play). In a particular example, the scope of a EULA may be defined to include not only offline campaigns or portions of game video, but also online components such as multiplayer modes and features. In some instances, game updates such as patches and expansion packs may include their own separate EULA, which may be used as a vehicle to reapply or update the EULA of the previous game or games. For example, a software developer may condition installation of the new game data on the end-user's acceptance of the new EULA.

The preamble is typically followed by a section or clause specifying the allowable actions by the end-user with respect to the game or other piece of software. The EULA shown in Figure 1, for example, permits the end-user to install and use the video game. In some instances, the EULA may place conditions upon the permitted actions such as requiring that the operating system upon which the video game is installed is validly licensed. The scope of the license may further define whether an end-user is permitted to make copies and if so, the number of copies that may be made and an allowable purpose for those copies. As one can appreciate, the scope of the license grant may be carved out to be very specific if the software developer chooses to do so. With very few exceptions, most uses, copies, and/or distributions of the software may be contracted around.

In some instances, the first section (e.g., the Grant of License section) is used only to notify the end-user of his or her right to use, install, and/or copy the game. Other rights and obligations may be defined in a subsequent section such as the Description of Other Rights and Limitations as shown in Figure 1. However, there is no required format for the EULA. Logic and flow should control how the various clauses and sections of your EULA are organized. In the sample EULA, the Description of Other Rights and Limitations defines actions that the end-user is not permitted to take. For example, the EULA may prevent an end-user from disassembling, decompiling, and/or reverse-engineering the software. Other types of limitations may include restrictions on distribution, removal of copyright notices, and rental. The scope of the restrictions and limitations may be broadened to cover not only the current version of the software, but also future additions and/or other modifications. For example, the EULA may define limitations on future aspects of the software such as support software, additional game data, game fixes, and patches.

Perhaps one of the more important clauses or sections of a EULA is the termination clause. The termination clause defines the conditions under which the software developer may revoke or otherwise terminate the license granted by the EULA. Additionally, the termination clause may specify obligations of the user upon termination (e.g., destruction of all copies of the software). While the sample termination clause illustrated in Figure 1 allows the software developer to terminate the license if the end-user fails to comply with any of the terms of the EULA, other even broader termination clauses are possible. In some cases, the termination clause may provide the software developer with a virtual carte blanche in revoking or terminating an end-user's license. The following is an example of an even broader termination clause:

> We reserve the right to transfer or cease the operation of the Game at any time or to terminate your license to the Software and your access to the Game at any time, without notice or refund, for any reason whatsoever, including, without limitation, as a result of your breach of this EULA, the Code of Conduct, or the Terms of Service, if we are unable to verify or authenticate any information you provide to us, or if we discontinue offering the Game.[3]

Copyright clauses are commonly included in EULAs to cover all copyrights and other intellectual property rights (other than the copyright in the game itself) that may be included in the game. For example, separate and distinct copyrights may subsist in the images, music, or other audio and compilations of data that may form one or more parts of the video game. To avoid any potential dispute as to copyright ownership or the existence of a license to use these separate copyrights, the copyright clause will specifically and unequivocally state that such other copyrights are owned by the software developer or content owner and that no license is granted to use these separate copyrights outside of the game. Accordingly, while the end-user is granted a license to use the game as a whole, the user might not have the right to use the individual game parts such as specific characters, graphical control elements, music, and background art outside of the game.

In some instances, warranties may automatically exist and attach to a product or service unless it is specifically disclaimed. The warranty clause or section of the EULA is the key to a software developer avoiding unwanted or unintended warranties from being claimed by the end-user. The sample warranty clause of the EULA illustrated in Figure 1 is a relatively straightforward and all-encompassing disclaimer of warranties. Warranty clauses will vary; for example, EULAs for some games may provide a warranty against defects of the physical storage media on which the software is sold (e.g., CD-ROMs, DVD-ROMS, etc.). If you choose to provide a warranty, it is important to make sure that the duration of the warranty is specifically defined. Note that in some jurisdictions, certain types of warranties such as implied warranties cannot be disclaimed. However, you may be able to limit the duration of such warranties, again depending on the jurisdiction.

---

3. Source: End-User License Agreement for *Lord of the Rings Online*® (http://www.lotro.com/support /policies/218-eula).

In addition to reservation of termination rights and disclaiming or limiting unintended warranties, you, as a software developer, will also want to make sure that you have disclaimed any potential liability arising from various causes. As shown in the EULA in Figure 1, some typical sources of liability include libel, infringements of rights of publicity, privacy, trademark rights, business interruption, personal injury, loss of privacy, moral rights, or the disclosure of confidential information, data loss, and lost profits. While the ability to limit your liability will vary from jurisdiction to jurisdiction, it is usually better to be on the safe side and be overinclusive in disclaiming potential sources of liability, rather than possibly underestimating them.

The above provides a brief description of sections and clauses that are found in a typical EULA. Other terms may be defined depending on a variety of factors including the type of game (e.g., online vs. offline) and features of the game. For example, massively multiplayer online games (MMOGs) may include a cheating clause that conditions the license on the user agreeing not to use third-party software to alter or modify the game play. An example of an anticheating clause is shown below:

> Except as expressly permitted by {Insert Company name} by written notice (and in such event in accordance with {Insert Company name} specified restrictions and guidelines), you may not use any third-party software to interact with the Game or change game play in the Game. The Game may be played only through authorized Servers maintained by {Insert Company name} or its subcontractors. You may not create or provide any other means through which the Game may be played by others, including, without limitation, through server emulators (which emulate or contain unauthorized copies of the Server). You may not take any action that imposes an unreasonable or disproportionately large load on our servers or other infrastructure.[4]

Other types of EULA clauses include agreements on the part of the end-user to allow the software developer or a distributor to send e-mails to the end-user, definitions of player conduct during use of the game, and rights to amend the EULA with or without notice. You can probably think of a million other types of clauses that may be added to such an agreement. Whether your EULA should ultimately include the clauses described in this section or other potential licensing terms will depend largely on your needs and the specific attributes of your game.

---

4. Source: End-User License Agreement for *Lord of the Rings Online*® (retrieved from http://www.lotro .com/support/policies/218-eula).

» PRIVACY POLICIES

With the skyrocketing popularity of Facebook, Twitter, MySpace, and other social networking sites, one might wonder if privacy still exists or if anyone out there still cares about privacy. It does and they do. In fact, the misappropriation of personal information may cost a software developer significant headaches (read: money) if not competently addressed ahead of time. Privacy policies are generally the choice legal instrument by which companies will define their collection, use, dissemination, and protection of personal information. While privacy policies are not required by federal law, the Federal Trade Commission (FTC) has set forth recommended guidelines for fair use of information. Privacy policies or statements also serve the purpose of limiting a software developer's liability in this arena by securing the user's advance agreement to the collection, use, and security of personal information. For example, similar to EULA practice, the software developer will usually require that the end-user accept the terms of the privacy policy before installing a game, using a service associated with the game, and/or accessing and viewing supplemental game information (e.g., community forums, websites, etc.). Portions of a sample privacy statement are shown in Figure 2 (a copy of the below sample is included on the attached CD).

Figure 2 Sample Privacy Policy

PRIVACY STATEMENT
{Insert Company Name} Privacy Statement
(Last updated {Insert Date})

The {Insert Company Name} Websites consisting of {Insert Website Domain}, {Insert Any Website Names} are operated by {Insert Company Name} or its suppliers (the "Websites"). This Privacy Statement applies to the Website you are currently viewing and describes what information is collected and used on this Website. By using the Websites, you consent to the data practices described in this Statement.

COLLECTION OF YOUR PERSONAL INFORMATION
The use of the Websites does not require you to disclose any personal information. However, the sites offer you the opportunity to register for an account, which permits you to use additional features offered on the Websites, including Communities, Forums, and the Store. Should you choose to register for an account you will be asked for personal information such as your name and e-mail address. You may also be asked for additional personal information should you choose to subscribe to newsletters or enter sweepstakes.

If you are a subscriber of the {Insert Subscription Service Name}, your game handle(s), nickname(s), and statistics such as high scores may be displayed on {Insert Web Domain}; and your online presence will be visible to those on your friends list.

{Insert Company Name} may collect information about your visit, including the pages you view, the links you click, and other actions taken within the site. We also collect certain standard information that your browser sends to every Website you visit, such as your IP address, browser type and language, access times, and referring Website addresses.

USE OF YOUR PERSONAL INFORMATION

{Insert Company Name} uses the personal information it collects on the Sites to operate the sites and deliver the services you have requested. For example, when you subscribe to a newsletter, we use your e-mail address to send you the newsletter(s) you have requested. If you choose to enter your name and postal address, we will use that information for future mailings from {Insert Company Name} about {Insert Company Name} news and promotions. We use geographical location to determine what localized information {Insert Company Name} should provide customers. When you choose to enter a sweepstakes, we use your contact information in order to be able to contact you in the event you are a winner of the sweepstakes.

We occasionally hire other companies to provide limited services on our behalf, such as sending newsletters, answering customer questions, fulfilling requests, and performing statistical analysis of our services. We will provide those companies only the information they need to deliver the service, and they are prohibited from using that information for any other purpose. We may provide your personal information to {Insert Any Related or Partner Companies} in connection with our administration of the Websites and/or {Insert Company Name} or {Insert Related or Partner Companies} games, including without limitation, for the purpose of enforcing the Terms of Use terms.

{Insert Company Name} may disclose your personal information, without notice if required to do so by law or in the good faith belief that such action is necessary to: (a) conform to the edicts of the law or comply with legal process served on {Insert Company Name}, or its suppliers and publishers; (b) protect and defend the rights or property of {Insert Company Name} or its suppliers and publishers; and (c) protect the personal safety of {Insert Company Name} employees or agents, users of {Insert Company Name} products or services, or members of the public, and (d) protect the integrity of the online community on the Website and games.

Personal information that you provide on {Insert Web Domain} may be stored and processed in the United States or any other country in which {Insert Company Name and/or Other Companies} or its affiliates, subsidiaries, suppliers, publishers, or agents maintain facilities. By using the Websites, you consent to any such transfer of information outside of your country.

{Insert Company Name and/or Other Companies} keeps track of the pages on this Website that our customers visit in order to determine which areas of the site are the most popular. This data is used to deliver customized content and advertising within {Insert Company Name} to customers whose behavior indicates that they are interested in a particular subject area.

CONTROL OF YOUR PERSONAL INFORMATION
You may unsubscribe to newsletters by following the instructions in the newsletter you receive. If your e-mail address has changed and you would like to continue to receive newsletters, you will need to sign up again for the newsletter on this Website with your new e-mail address.

{Insert Web Domain} may send out periodic e-mails informing you of technical service issues, product surveys, new feature announcements, and other news about {Insert Company Name} and other related products and services. These e-mails are considered essential to the provision of the service you have requested. You will not be able to choose to unsubscribe to these mailings, as they are considered a part of the service you have chosen.

Please be aware that this Privacy Statement and the choices you make on this site may not apply to personal information you may have provided to {Insert Company Name and/or Other Companies} in the context of other separately operated {Insert Company Name and/or Other Companies} products or services.

SECURITY OF YOUR PERSONAL INFORMATION
{Insert Company Name} is committed to protecting the security of your personal information. We use a variety of security technologies and procedures to help protect your personal information from unauthorized access, use, or disclosure. For example, we store the personal information you provide on computer servers with limited access that are located in controlled facilities.

If you choose to create a profile on a Website you will be required to select a password. This password can be changed once you have logged into the service. It is your responsibility to keep your password confidential. Do not share this information with anyone. If you are sharing a computer with anyone you should always choose to log out before leaving the Website to protect access to your information from subsequent users.

USE OF COOKIES

{Insert Company Name} uses cookies to help you personalize your online experience. A cookie is a text file that is placed on your hard disk by a web page server. Cookies cannot be used to run programs or deliver viruses to your computer. Cookies are uniquely assigned to you, and can be read only by a web server in the domain that issued the cookie to you.

One of the primary purposes of cookies is to provide a convenience feature to save you time. The purpose of a cookie is to tell the web server that you have returned to a specific page, so that when you visit the site again, the experience will be personalized. You have the ability to accept or decline cookies. Most Web browsers automatically accept cookies, but you can usually modify your browser setting to decline cookies if you prefer. If you choose to set your computer to accept cookies from the Websites, you may also choose to be logged into the site automatically. You may also select a country of your choice as your default home page. This selection is stored in a cookie. If you choose to decline cookies, you may not be able to fully experience the interactive features of the Websites or the other Websites you visit.

COMMUNITIES AND FORUMS OFFERED ON THIS WEBSITE

Please keep in mind that if you directly disclose personally identifiable information or personally sensitive data through Communities, Forums, Messages, or other public online forums, this information may be collected and used by others. We recommend that you be cautious in giving out personal information to others in these public online forums.

CHANGES TO THIS STATEMENT

This Privacy Statement applies only to the Websites and not other companies or organizations to which we may provide links from this Website. {Insert Company Name} will occasionally update this Privacy Statement. When we do, we will also revise the "last updated" date at the top of the privacy statement. For material changes to this Statement, {Insert Company Name} will notify you by placing prominent notice on the Website. We encourage you to periodically review this Privacy Statement to be informed of how {Insert Company Name} is protecting your information.

CONTACT INFORMATION

{Insert Company Name} welcomes your comments regarding this Privacy Statement. If at any time you believe that the Websites have not adhered to this Privacy Statement, please notify us and we will use all commercially reasonable efforts to promptly determine and correct the problem.

If you have questions regarding this statement or require additional information, please contact us.

{Insert Contact Information}

Source: Based on Privacy Policy for Bungie.net (retrieved from http://www.bungie.net/help/privacy_statement .aspx)

Your privacy policy should include at least four main sections: collection, use, control, and security of personal information. The collection section, for instance, should be used to introduce the user to the ways in which the game or website may collect personal information. You may also choose not only to indicate whether personal information is collected, but to also note any advantages and benefits derived from collecting the personal data. For example, in the sample collection policy in Figure 2, the policy is careful to indicate that collection of personal information is not required, but it goes on to explain that collection may allow the user to take advantage of other features, offers, and benefits of the sites. For full disclosure, it is also good practice to identify other types of information that are collected through the game or site that may or may not technically fall under "personal information" (e.g., IP addresses, pages viewed, links selected).

As its name indicates, the use of personal information portion of a privacy statement should identify the potential uses of the user's personal information including internal and external uses. For example, uses may include storage, sale to third parties or other distribution, localization of content, operation of contests, compliance with federal, state, or local laws, and/or enforcement of terms of use or the EULA. Again, this section of the privacy policy should be overinclusive to avoid potential complaints that an end-user was not advised of a particular use of his or her personal information and potential liabilities resulting therefrom.

Control of personal information refers to the amount of control the end-user has in the collection and use of his or her personal information. For example, you may offer the end-user ways to opt out of newsletters and other e-mails or options to prevent personal information from being distributed to third parties. These options should be identified in the privacy policy to at least prevent a user from claiming no knowledge or notice of options to control the use or collection of personal information. If applicable, it is also important to note that controls relating to one service, game, or site may not apply to another service, game, or site. Be careful to not overpromise. Mention only those controls that you are sure are or will be available to the user.

Other aspects to consider included in the privacy policy are provisions relating to cookies, provisions relating to communities and forums, and clauses relating to changes to the privacy policy itself. An important point of community and forum provisions is the notification that any personal information posted or submitted by the user may be freely collected and used by the company, third parties, and/or other users. You do not want a user to believe that he or she may directly post personal information with the expectation that the company operating the website, forums, or community will protect that information from collection, dissemination, and other uses.

Again, privacy policies are optional, unless you market your game to users under 13 years old (see the COPPA discussion in Chapter 7), but they do offer certain protections against claims against the service or software provider for misappropriation of personal data. In addition, privacy policies provide the user with a sense that you are aware of and are sensitive to the end-user's privacy concerns. Also note that many organizations such as the Entertainment Software Rating Board (ESRB) offer privacy policy certification programs. Such certification may lend further credence to a service or software provider's awareness of privacy issues.

» TERMS OF USE AGREEMENTS

With the growth of Internet gaming and cloud computing, end-users are increasingly consuming content stored on remote web servers rather than the user's own local machines. Even single-player games often have websites and forums hosted by software developers and filled with resources and content for end-users. To control how users may interact with these kinds of content, developers are more frequently using terms of use agreements (TOUs), which spell out the terms governing the use of web content and web software.

Figure 3 illustrates a sample terms of use agreement (TOU) (a copy of the sample is included on the attached CD).

Figure 3 Sample Terms of Use Agreement

TERMS OF USE AGREEMENT
(Last updated [Insert Date])
The {Insert Company Name} Website is composed of various Web pages, including {Insert Any Website Names/Domains} operated by {Insert Company Name} ("Company") (the "Websites").

The Websites are offered to you conditioned on your acceptance without modification of the terms, conditions, and notices contained herein. Your use of the Websites constitutes your agreement to all such terms, conditions, and notices. Your use of the Websites is also governed by the Privacy Statement, which is available at {Insert URL}, and incorporated by reference into these terms. The Websites may also contain additional terms that govern particular features or offers (for example, sweepstakes, contests, or chat areas) ("Additional Terms").

In the event that any of the terms, conditions, and notices contained herein conflict with the Additional Terms or other terms and guidelines contained within the Websites, then these terms shall control.

MODIFICATION OF THESE TERMS OF USE
{Company} reserves the right to change the terms, conditions, and notices under which the Websites are offered, including but not limited to the charges, if any, associated with the use of the Websites. You are responsible for regularly reviewing these terms and conditions and your continued use of the Websites acknowledges your agreement.

PERSONAL AND NONCOMMERCIAL USE LIMITATION
Unless otherwise specified, the Websites are for your personal and noncommercial use. You may not modify, copy, distribute, transmit, display, perform, reproduce, publish, license, create derivative works from, transfer, or sell any information, software, products, or services obtained from the Websites.

LINKS TO THIRD-PARTY SITES
The Websites may contain links to other Websites ("Linked Sites"). The Linked Sites are not under the control of {Insert Company Name} and {Insert Company Name} is not responsible for the contents of any Linked Site, including without limitation any link contained in a Linked Site, or any changes or updates to a Linked Site. {Insert Company Name} is not responsible for webcasting or any other form of transmission received from any Linked Site. {Insert Company Name} is providing these links to you only as a convenience,

and the inclusion of any link does not imply endorsement by {Insert Company Name} of the site or any association with its operators.

NO UNLAWFUL OR PROHIBITED USE

As a condition of your use of the Websites, you warrant to {Insert Company Name} that you will not use the Websites for any purpose that is unlawful or prohibited by these terms, conditions, and notices. You may not use the Websites in any manner which could damage, disable, overburden, or impair the Websites or interfere with any other party's use and enjoyment of the Websites. You may not obtain or attempt to obtain any materials or information through any means not intentionally made available or provided for through the Websites.

USE OF COMMUNICATION SERVICES

The Websites may contain bulletin board services, chat areas, news groups, forums, communities, personal web pages, calendars, and/or other message or communication facilities designed to enable you to communicate with the public at large or with a group (collectively, "Communication Services"). You agree to use the Communication Services only to post, send, and receive messages and material that are proper and related to the particular Communication Service. By way of example, and not as a limitation, you agree that when using a Communication Service, you will not:

Defame, abuse, harass, stalk, threaten, or otherwise violate the legal rights (such as rights of privacy and publicity) of others.

Publish, post, upload, distribute, or disseminate any inappropriate, profane, defamatory, infringing, obscene, indecent, or unlawful topic, name, material, or information.

Upload files that contain software or other material protected by intellectual property laws (or by rights of privacy of publicity) unless you own or control the rights thereto or have received all necessary consents.

Upload files that contain viruses, corrupted files, or any other similar software or programs that may damage the operation of another's computer.

Advertise or offer to sell or buy any goods or services for any business purpose, unless such Communication Service specifically allows such messages.

Conduct or forward surveys, contests, pyramid schemes, or chain letters.

Download any file posted by another user of a Communication Service that you know, or reasonably should know, cannot be legally distributed in such manner.

Falsify or delete any author attributions, legal or other proper notices, or proprietary designations or labels of the origin or source of software or other material contained in a file that is uploaded.

Restrict or inhibit any other user from using and enjoying the Communication Services.

Violate any code of conduct or other guidelines that may be applicable for any particular Communication Service.

Harvest or otherwise collect information about others, including e-mail addresses, without their consent.

Violate any applicable laws or regulations.

{Insert Company Name} has no obligation to monitor the Communication Services. However, {Insert Company Name} reserves the right to review materials posted to a Communication Service and to remove any materials in its sole discretion. {Insert Company Name} reserves the right to terminate your access to any or all of the Communication Services at any time without notice for any reason whatsoever.

{Insert Company Name} reserves the right at all times to disclose any information as necessary to satisfy any applicable law, regulation, legal process, or governmental request, or to edit, refuse to post, or to remove any information or materials, in whole or in part, in {Company's} sole discretion.

Always use caution when giving out any personally identifying information about yourself or your children in any Communication Service. {Insert Company Name} does not control or endorse the content, messages, or information found in any Communication Service and, therefore, {Insert Company Name} expressly disclaims any liability with regard to the Communication Services and any actions resulting from your participation in any Communication Service. Managers and hosts are not authorized {Company} spokespersons, and their views do not necessarily reflect those of {Insert Company Name}.

Materials uploaded to a Communication Service may be subject to posted limitations on usage, reproduction, and/or dissemination, and you are responsible for adhering to such limitations if you download the materials.

Additionally, by using the Websites you agree to comply with the Code of Conduct {if you desire to include one—see above}, which is available at {Insert URL}, and incorporated by reference into these terms.

MATERIALS PROVIDED TO {Company} OR POSTED AT ANY WEBSITE

{Insert Company Name} does not claim ownership of the materials you provide to {Insert Company Name} (including feedback and suggestions) or post, upload, input, or submit to any Website or its associated services (collectively "Submissions"), to the extent that what you post does not include materials provided to you or otherwise owned by {Insert Company Name} or its licensees. However, by posting, uploading, inputting, providing, or submitting your Submission you are granting {Insert Company Name}, its affiliated companies, and sublicensees permission to use your Submission in connection with the operation of their businesses including, without limitation, the rights to copy, distribute, transmit, publicly display, publicly perform, reproduce, edit, translate, and reformat your Submission and to publish your name in connection with your Submission.

No compensation will be paid with respect to the use of your Submission, as provided herein. {Insert Company Name} is under no obligation to post or use any Submission you may provide and may remove any Submission at any time in {Company's} sole discretion.

By posting, uploading, inputting, providing, or submitting your Submission you warrant and represent that you own or otherwise control all of the rights to your Submission as described in this section including, without limitation, all the rights necessary for you to provide, post, upload, input, or submit the Submissions (excluding materials provided to you by {Insert Company Name} for the purpose of making your Submission).

SOFTWARE AVAILABLE ON THE WEBSITES

Software (if any) that is made available to download from the Websites, excluding software that may be made available by end-users through a Communication Service ("Software"), is the copyrighted work of {Insert Company Name} and/or its suppliers and publishers. Your use of the Software is governed by the terms of the end-user license agreement, if any, that accompanies or is included with the Software ("License Agreement"). You may not install or use any Software that is accompanied by or includes a License Agreement unless you first agree to the License Agreement terms. For any Software not accompanied by a license agreement, {Insert Company Name} hereby grants to you, the user, a personal, nontransferable license to use the Software for viewing and otherwise using the particular Websites in accordance with these Terms of Use, and for no other purpose provided that you keep intact all copyright and other proprietary notices. All Software is owned by {Insert Company Name} and/or its suppliers and publishers and is protected by copyright laws and international treaty provisions. Any reproduction or redistribution of the Software is expressly prohibited by law, and may result in severe civil and criminal penalties. Violators will be prosecuted to the maximum extent possible. WITHOUT LIMITING THE FOREGOING, COPYING OR REPRODUCTION OF THE SOFTWARE TO ANY OTHER SERVER OR LOCATION FOR FURTHER REPRODUCTION OR REDISTRIBUTION IS EXPRESSLY PROHIBITED. THE SOFTWARE IS WARRANTED, IF AT ALL, ONLY ACCORDING TO THE TERMS OF THE LICENSE AGREEMENT. You acknowledge that the Software, and any accompanying documentation and/or technical information, is subject to applicable export control laws and regulations of the USA. You agree not to export or re-export the Software, directly or indirectly, to any countries that are subject to USA export restrictions.

LIABILITY DISCLAIMER

THE INFORMATION, SOFTWARE, PRODUCTS, AND SERVICES INCLUDED IN OR AVAILABLE THROUGH THE WEBSITES MAY INCLUDE INACCURACIES OR TYPOGRAPHICAL ERRORS. CHANGES ARE PERIODICALLY ADDED TO THE INFORMATION HEREIN. {Insert Company Name} AND/OR ITS RESPECTIVE SUPPLIERS MAY MAKE IMPROVEMENTS AND/OR CHANGES IN THE WEBSITES AT ANY TIME. ADVICE RECEIVED VIA THE WEBSITES SHOULD NOT BE RELIED UPON FOR PERSONAL, MEDICAL, LEGAL, OR FINANCIAL DECISIONS AND YOU SHOULD CONSULT AN APPROPRIATE PROFESSIONAL FOR SPECIFIC ADVICE TAILORED TO YOUR SITUATION.

{Insert Company Name} AND/OR ITS RESPECTIVE SUPPLIERS AND PUBLISHERS MAKE NO REPRESENTATIONS ABOUT THE SUITABILITY, RELIABILITY, AVAILABILITY, TIMELINESS, AND ACCURACY OF THE INFORMATION, SOFTWARE, PRODUCTS, SERVICES, AND RELATED GRAPHICS CONTAINED ON THE WEBSITES FOR ANY PURPOSE. ALL SUCH INFORMATION, SOFTWARE, PRODUCTS, SERVICES, AND RELATED GRAPHICS ARE PROVIDED "AS IS" WITHOUT WARRANTY OF ANY KIND. {Insert Company Name} AND/OR ITS RESPECTIVE SUPPLIERS AND PUBLISHERS HEREBY DISCLAIM ALL WARRANTIES AND CONDITIONS WITH REGARD TO THIS INFORMATION, SOFTWARE, PRODUCTS, SERVICES, AND RELATED GRAPHICS, INCLUDING ALL IMPLIED WARRANTIES AND CONDITIONS OF MERCHANTABILITY, FITNESS FOR A PARTICULAR PURPOSE, TITLE, AND NONINFRINGEMENT.

IN NO EVENT SHALL {Insert Company Name} AND/OR ITS SUPPLIERS OR PUBLISHERS BE LIABLE FOR ANY DIRECT, INDIRECT, PUNITIVE, INCIDENTAL, SPECIAL, OR CONSEQUENTIAL DAMAGES, OR ANY DAMAGES WHATSOEVER INCLUDING, WITHOUT LIMITATION, DAMAGES FOR LOSS OF USE, DATA, OR PROFITS, ARISING OUT OF OR IN ANY WAY CONNECTED WITH THE USE OR PERFORMANCE OF THE WEBSITES, WITH THE DELAY OR INABILITY TO USE THE WEBSITES OR RELATED SERVICES, THE PROVISION OF OR FAILURE TO PROVIDE SERVICES, OR FOR ANY INFORMATION, SOFTWARE, PRODUCTS, SERVICES AND RELATED GRAPHICS OBTAINED THROUGH THE WEBSITES, OR OTHERWISE ARISING OUT OF THE USE OF THE WEBSITES, WHETHER BASED ON CONTRACT, TORT, NEGLIGENCE, STRICT LIABILITY, OR OTHERWISE, EVEN IF {Insert Company Name} OR ANY OF ITS SUPPLIERS OR PUBLISHERS HAS BEEN ADVISED OF THE POSSIBILITY OF DAMAGES. BECAUSE SOME STATES/JURISDICTIONS DO NOT ALLOW THE EXCLUSION OR LIMITATION OF LIABILITY FOR CONSEQUENTIAL OR INCIDENTAL DAMAGES, THE ABOVE LIMITATION MAY NOT APPLY TO YOU. IF YOU ARE DISSATISFIED WITH ANY PORTION OF THE WEBSITES OR WITH ANY OF THESE TERMS OF USE, YOUR SOLE AND EXCLUSIVE REMEDY IS TO DISCONTINUE USING THE WEBSITES.

TERMINATION/ACCESS RESTRICTION
{Insert Company Name} reserves the right, in its sole discretion, to terminate your access to any or all Websites and the related services or any portion thereof at any time, without notice.

GENERAL
This agreement is governed by the laws of the State of {Insert Your Desired State—e.g., the state in which your Company's headquarters are located}, U.S.A. You hereby consent to the exclusive jurisdiction and venue of courts in {Insert City/County/etc.}, {Insert State}, U.S.A., in all disputes arising out of or relating to the use of the Websites. You agree that no joint venture, partnership, employment, or agency relationship exists between you and {Insert Company Name} as a result of this agreement or use of the Websites. {Company's} performance of this agreement is subject to existing laws and legal process, and nothing contained in this agreement is in derogation of {Company's} right to comply with governmental, court, and law enforcement requests or requirements relating to your use of the Websites or information provided to or gathered by {Insert Company Name} with respect to such use. If any part of this agreement is determined to be invalid or unenforceable pursuant

to applicable law including, but not limited to, the warranty disclaimers and liability limitations set forth above, then the invalid or unenforceable provision will be deemed superseded by a valid, enforceable provision that most closely matches the intent of the original provision and the remainder of the agreement shall continue in effect. Unless otherwise specified herein, this agreement constitutes the entire agreement between the user and {Insert Company Name} with respect to the Websites and it supersedes all prior or contemporaneous communications and proposals, whether electronic, oral, or written, between the user and {Insert Company Name} with respect to the Websites. A printed version of this agreement and of any notice given in electronic form shall be admissible in judicial or administrative proceedings based upon or relating to this agreement to the same extent and subject to the same conditions as other business documents and records originally generated and maintained in printed form.

COPYRIGHT AND TRADEMARK NOTICES
All contents of the Websites are Copyright © {Insert Company Name} and/or its suppliers. All rights reserved.

TRADEMARKS. {Insert Company and Product Trademarks} and/or other related products referenced herein are either trademarks or registered trademarks of {Insert Company Name} or its suppliers. The names of actual companies and products mentioned herein may be the trademarks of their respective owners.

The example companies, organizations, products, people, and events depicted herein are fictitious. No association with any real company, organization, product, person, or event is intended or should be inferred.

Any rights not expressly granted herein are reserved.

NOTICES AND PROCEDURE FOR MAKING CLAIMS OF COPYRIGHT INFRINGEMENT
Pursuant to Title 17, United States Code, Section 512(c)(2), notifications of claimed copyright infringement should be sent to Service Provider's Designated Agent. ALL INQUIRIES NOT RELEVANT TO THE FOLLOWING PROCEDURE WILL RECEIVE NO RESPONSE. If you believe that your work has been posted on a Website in a way that constitutes copyright infringement, please contact {Insert Company Name} at the address below and provide the following information: (1) an electronic or physical signature of the person authorized to act on behalf of the owner of the copyright interest; (2) a

description of the copyrighted work that you claim has been infringed, and identification of the URL or other specific location on the Site where the material that you claim is infringing is located; (3) your address, telephone number, and e-mail address; (4) a statement by you that you have a good faith belief that the disputed use is not authorized by the copyright owner, its agent, or the law; and (5) a statement by you, made under penalty of perjury, that the above information in your notice is accurate and that you are the copyright owner or authorized to act on the copyright owner's behalf.

{Company's} designated agent for notice of copyright infringement can be reached at:

{Insert Company Name, Contact Person Name or Title, and Mailing Address}

Source: Terms of Use provided by Bungie.net (retrieved from http://www.bungie.net/help/terms_of_use.aspx).

As seen in Figure 3, a TOU may include a variety of sections and may begin by identifying the content that it governs—websites, message boards, streaming content, downloadable software, and so on. In addition, the TOU may reference the EULA and/or the Privacy Policy, as all of these agreements may work together in defining acceptable and unacceptable use of the software and web content.

Planning Ahead for Future Changes to the TOU

Inevitably, your website and web content will change, and when that happens, you might want or need to update your TOU as well. Accordingly, your TOU should reserve the right to modify the terms and conditions that govern an end-user's ability to use your web content, and your TOU may place the obligation on your end-users to review these terms and conditions on a regular basis, as the sample TOU in Figure 3 does. In addition, unless you plan to implement a click-wrap regime where a user must affirmatively assent to the TOU each time it is updated, you may wish for your TOU to assert that continued use of the web content or web software constitutes agreement to the TOU. This type of provision may help you down the road when you might need to prove that a user agreed to the terms included in the TOU.

Including Use Limitations

As seen in the sample TOU agreement illustrated in Figure 3, a TOU may include a variety of restrictions on the use of various aspects of a website and/or other content. For example, the TOU may include a provision requiring the end-user to use the web content for personal and noncommercial uses only. In addition, and somewhat for your own protection, the TOU may include a provision requiring the end-user to agree not to use your website or related content for illegal purposes. Along these lines, the TOU also may include provisions requiring the end-user not to damage your website or content, not to prevent others from accessing your website or content (e.g., by requiring the end-user to agree not to disable or overburden your servers via a denial of service attack), or not to hack into your servers.

While it may seem that some of these provisions are unnecessary (especially to the extent that they overlap with computer crime laws that already exist), it is nevertheless beneficial to include them in your TOU. After all, if someone does take down your website with a denial of service attack, you may be able to later sue them (and recover damages) on a breach-of-contract theory based on the TOU in addition to traditional tort and property theories of legal liability.

Besides these use restrictions, your TOU might also include restrictions on how an end-user might interact with other users on your website (e.g., via message boards, forums, and chat rooms). As seen in the sample TOU illustrated in Figure 3, you may require your users to agree to a lot of provisions that are grounded in common sense. For instance, you may require your users not to harass or abuse other users, post infringing or adult content, upload files infected with viruses, use your message boards to post advertisements or further fraudulent schemes, collect e-mail addresses of other users, and so on. You may also use this opportunity in your TOU to reserve your rights to review, modify, and/ or remove anything posted to any of your websites for any reason and perhaps even set out some kind of "Code of Conduct" with which you desire your users to comply while using your website.

Another issue you might wish to address in your TOU is the limitations you may want to place on software downloaded from your website. For example, you may explain in the TOU that software downloaded from your website may be used only in accordance with the terms of your EULA, as seen in the sample TOU illustrated in Figure 3. Additionally, you might want to restrict users from downloading software from your website and reposting such software to their own website to host it for others. Because the TOU addresses your website and associated content, the TOU is a good place to include these kinds of terms.

Protecting Yourself with Disclaimers

In addition to using the TOU to limit the ways in which end-users can use your website and other web content, you may also want to use the TOU to limit your own liability when it comes to how end-users interact with your website and web content.

For example, as seen in the example TOU illustrated in Figure 3, you may want to include a few provisions in your TOU that address how you can use content that users might post or upload to your website. In particular, you may want to spell out in your TOU that even if you do not own the content that a user has posted or uploaded to your website, by posting or uploading such content, the user has agreed to let you use, distribute, copy, modify, and so on whatever it is that the user posted. In addition, you might also specify that the user's name may be published in connection with the post or upload—again, just to protect yourself in case the user later asserts that you have used his or her name without permission.

Other issues that you might want to address with respect to content that is posted or uploaded by users include compensation and ownership. Specifically, you probably want to explain that users are not entitled to get paid for posting or uploading things to your website (unless your business model does involve paying end-users). In addition, and even though you already might have spelled this out elsewhere, you may want to repeat yourself and state that by posting or uploading something to your website, users are agreeing that they have the right to do so—after all, you probably do not want your users to turn your message boards into an illegal file-sharing exchange.

Besides dealing with issues related to content posted or uploaded by users, you might also want to address other liability issues that could arise. For example, you may wish to include provisions disclaiming your liability for content hosted by third parties that your website links to. In addition, you may wish to include a general legal disclaimer that explains that you will not be liable for things like breaches of warranty, reliance damages, consequential damages, and so on arising out of a user's use of (or inability to use) your website and other web content. Bear in mind, however, that even if you include a broad disclaimer like the one that appears in the sample TOU illustrated in Figure 3, various contract and tort laws might render some (if not all) of your attempted disclaimer provisions invalid. Nevertheless, in some states, when portions of a broad disclaimer are invalid because of existing laws, the remaining valid portions of the disclaimer are still enforceable.

Another provision that you might consider including in your TOU is a termination of access provision like the one included in the sample TOU. Essentially, you will probably want to reserve the right to ban any particular user from accessing and using your website and other web content for any reason you like.

Other provisions that you might want to include in your TOU include general legal provisions, as seen in the sample TOU illustrated in Figure 3. For example, you may want to include "choice of law" provisions specifying that any dispute arising out of the agreement or out of the use of your website or web content will be adjudicated in your local jurisdiction and/or submitted to arbitration. A provision like this might save you time and money down the road if and when a dispute does arise, because it might be able to keep you from having to travel across the country to appear in court. You also may wish to include provisions dealing with severability, which as discussed above, may allow the remaining valid portions of your TOU to be enforced even if other portions of your TOU are invalidated and rendered unenforceable.

Addressing Some Remaining Issues Involving Copyrights and Trademarks

Because your TOU deals with your websites and web content, the TOU is also a good place to spell out your copyright and trademark rights in your websites and web content. A simple notice regarding each, as illustrated in the sample TOU illustrated in Figure 3, should suffice. Besides these notices, you may also want to include a general reservation of rights like the one included in the sample TOU.

Another issue you may wish to address in your TOU is the designation of an agent to receive notices of copyright infringement. Under the federal copyright laws, a service provider may be able to avoid liability in some situations where a user posts infringing content to the service provider's website, as long as the service provider complies with various elements of the statute—including designating an agent to receive notifications of alleged copyright infringement.[5] If you are going to host content that is posted or uploaded by users (e.g., on a forum or message board), you should review (and comply with) all of the requirements spelled out in the safe-harbor provisions of the copyright act (17 U.S.C. § 512(c)), in addition to designating an agent to receive notices of alleged copyright infringement in your TOU. For example, in order to take advantage of the safe-harbor provisions, service providers must have implemented and informed subscribers and account holders of the service provider's system or network of a policy that provides for the termination in appropriate circumstances of subscribers and account holders of the service provider's system or network who are repeat infringers. Service providers must also accommodate and not interfere with reasonable standard technical measures used by copyright owners to identify or protect copyrighted works.

A sample copyright policy addressing alleged content violations is shown below in Figure 4 and is included on the attached CD. The sample policy explains the procedure that service providers should follow to insulate themselves from claims of infringement by content owners when an end-user uploads copyrighted content to the service provider's network without authority of the content owner.

COPYRIGHT POLICY

[INSERT COMPANY NAME], its officers, employees, affiliates, subsidiaries, divisions, representatives, and agents acting on behalf of [INSERT COMPANY NAME] (collectively referred to herein as "We," "Us," "Our," and "ISP") respect others' intellectual property rights and request that the users of [INSERT URL] ("Web Site") do the same. All content, including copyrightable works, trademarks, service marks, and patentable inventions on the Web Site are the property of ISP unless explicitly stated otherwise. No right, title,

---

5. *See* 17 U.S.C. § 512(c)(2).

or interest to the content is granted by your use of the Web Site, other than a right to review the content using a conventional Internet browser (i.e., ordinary web browsing). Any other uses, including making copies of any content, are strictly prohibited.

In compliance with the Digital Millennium Copyright Act ("DMCA") at 17 U.S.C. § 512 et seq., ISP does not interfere with standard technical measures identifying and/or protecting copyrighted works and reserves the right to terminate any user account who is a repeat infringer of others' copyrights.

DMCA Notices: It is ISP's policy to respond to notices of alleged copyright infringement according to the DMCA. Regardless of whether or not ISP believes that it is liable for any copyright infringement for which we are provided notice, our response may include removing or disabling access to material claimed to be the subject of infringing activity and/or terminating subscriber access to the site, at our sole discretion and operating within the parameters of the DMCA as discussed below.

If you believe there is content on the site that infringes your copyright, you may submit a DMCA Notification of alleged copyright infringement by emailing the DMCA Notification to: address@domain.com, or by mailing the notice to:

ISP, Inc.
DMCA Content Manager
Address
City, State Zip

Any such DMCA Notification must include the following:
- Identification of the copyrighted work claimed to have been infringed or, if multiple copyrighted works are covered by a single notification, a representative list of such works.
- Identification of the material that is claimed to be infringing or to be the subject of infringing activity and that is requested to be removed or access to which is requested to be disabled, and information reasonably sufficient to permit ISP to locate the material.
- Information reasonably sufficient to permit ISP to contact you (i.e., the complaining party), such as an address, telephone number, and, if available, an electronic mail address at which you may be contacted.
- A statement that you have a good faith belief that use of the material in the manner complained of is not authorized by the copyright owner, its agent, or the law.

- A statement that the information in the notification is accurate, and **under penalty of perjury**, that you are authorized to act on behalf of the owner of an exclusive right that is allegedly infringed.
- A physical or electronic signature of a person authorized to act on behalf of the owner of an exclusive right that is allegedly infringed.

Upon receiving a DMCA Notification in compliance with the above, ISP will act to expeditiously remove, or disable access to, the material that is claimed to be infringing or to be the subject of infringing activity. If we remove or disable access in response to a DMCA Notification, we will make a good faith attempt to contact the owner or administrator of the affected content so that they can submit a DMCA Counter-Notification, if applicable. We may also document notices of alleged infringement on which we act, and provide copies of notices of alleged infringement to third parties, at our discretion.

If your content has been removed by us in response to our receipt of a DMCA Notification as outlined above, and you believe the removal was inappropriate, you may submit a DMCA Counter-Notification by emailing the DMCA Counter-Notification to: address@domain.com, or by mailing the notice to:

ISP, Inc.
DMCA Content Manager
Address
City, State Zip

Any such DMCA Counter-Notification must include the following:
- Identification of the material that has been removed or to which access has been disabled and the location at which the material appeared before it was removed or access to it was disabled.
- A statement **under penalty of perjury** that you have a good faith belief that the material was removed or disabled as a result of mistake or mis-identification of the material to be removed or disabled.
- Your name, address, and telephone number, and a statement that you consent to the jurisdiction of Federal District Court for the judicial district in which your address is located, or if your address is outside of the United States, for any judicial district for which jurisdiction for ISP would be appropriate, and that you will accept service of process from the person who submitted the DMCA notification or an agent of such person.
- A physical or electronic signature of the subscriber.

Upon receiving a DMCA Counter-Notification in compliance with the above, ISP will reasonably act to notify the person who provided the initial DMCA Notification with a copy of the DMCA Counter-Notification, and inform that person that ISP will replace the removed material or cease disabling access to it after 10 business days and no later than 14 business days. At such time, ISP will replace the removed material and cease disabling access to the removed material, unless we first receive notice from the person who submitted the initial DMCA Notification that such person has filed an action seeking a court order to restrain the alleged infringer from engaging in infringing activity relating to the material on the web site.

As you can see, there are all sorts of terms, conditions, and use limitations you might want to impose when it comes to how your website and web content are accessed and used. The provisions that you ultimately include in your legal policies likely will vary depending on the individual nature and requirements of your website and web content.

7

THE CHILDREN'S ONLINE PRIVACY PROTECTION ACT

By Ross Dannenberg

The Entertainment Software Association's *2010 Sales, Demographic and Usage Data* report indicates that 25 percent of all gamers are under the age of 18. What does this mean to you? Regardless of whether you are developing a massively multiplayer online game (MMOG), role-playing game (RPG), first-person shooter (FPS) game, or strategy, side-scroller, or a puzzle-based game, chances are that some kids will be interested in playing, and there are special considerations when kids are involved.

The Children's Online Privacy Protection Act, or COPPA, was enacted to place parents in control of what information is collected from their young children online. COPPA was designed to protect children under the age of 13 while accounting for the dynamic nature of the Internet. If you fall into one of the following two categories, then COPPA applies to you:

1. operators of commercial websites and online services *directed to children under 13* that collect, use, or disclose personal information from children, and
2. operators of general audience websites or online services with *actual knowledge* that they are collecting, using, or disclosing personal information from children under 13.

The first category—websites directed to children—is broader than it sounds. A website operator can't simply sit back and say "My game is for users 13 and older only" and expect to be immune from COPPA compliance. Whether a website is directed to children under 13 is determined based on criteria such as whether its subject matter and language are child-oriented, whether it uses animated characters, or whether advertising appearing on the website is directed to children. Empirical evidence regarding the actual and intended ages of the website's visitors also may be taken into account.

Keep in mind that the triggering event for COPPA is *collection of personal information* from a child under 13 years old. If you do not collect personal information from anyone under 13, then COPPA does not apply to you. However, the FTC recommends that all websites post privacy policies so visitors can easily learn about the website operator's information practices. Some surveys show that parents are uncomfortable with their children giving out any personal information online, so they may be pleased to read your privacy policy and discover that you do not collect personally identifiable information.

If you fall within one of the above two categories, then you must adhere to the following requirements:

1. Post a clear and comprehensive privacy policy on your website describing your information practices for children's personal information;
2. Provide direct notice to parents and obtain verifiable parental consent, with limited exceptions, before collecting personal information from children;
3. Give parents the choice of consenting to the operator's collection and internal use of a child's information while prohibiting the operator from disclosing that information to third parties;
4. Provide parents access to their child's personal information to review and/or have the information deleted;
5. Give parents the opportunity to prevent further use or online collection of a child's personal information; and
6. Maintain the confidentiality, security, and integrity of information you collect from children.

COPPA also prohibits operators from conditioning a child's participation in an online activity on the child's providing more information than is reasonably necessary to participate in that activity.

If you will be collecting information from users under 13 years old, you must comply with the above requirements, which includes posting your practices in your privacy policy. Your privacy policy should include the name, address, telephone number, and e-mail address of each operator collecting or maintaining personal information from children through your site; the types of personal information collected from children and whether it is collected actively or passively (e.g., do you use cookies, GUIDs, IP addresses?); how such personal information is or may be used; whether such personal information is disclosed to third parties, allowing parents to deny consent to disclosure of the collected information to third parties; that the operator cannot condition a child's participation in an activity on the disclosure of more information than is reasonably necessary to participate; and that the parent can review the child's personal information and refuse to permit the further collection or use of the child's information.

COPPA also requires that you place a clear and prominent link to your privacy policy on your home page and at each area where personal information is collected. Your privacy policy should be kept simple, too, because the COPPA rules require that privacy policies must be "clearly and understandably written, be complete, and contain no unrelated, confusing, or contradictory materials."

When obtaining parental consent, you can use any number of methods to obtain verifiable parental consent, as long as the method you choose is reasonably calculated to ensure that the person providing consent is, in fact, the child's parent. There are several options:

If you are going to disclose children's personal information to third parties, or make it publicly available through operation of an online service such as a social networking site, a blog-hosting service, personal home pages, chat rooms, message boards, pen pal services, or e-mail accounts, then you must use one of the more reliable methods to obtain verifiable parental consent enumerated in the rule:

- Provide a form for the parent to print, fill out, sign, and mail or fax back to you (the "print-and-send" method);
- Require the parent to use a credit card in connection with a transaction (which could consist of a membership or subscription fee, a purchase, or a charge to cover the cost of processing the credit card). The transaction must be completed;
- Maintain a toll-free telephone number staffed by trained personnel for parents to call in their consent; or
- Obtain consent through an e-mail from the parent, if that e-mail contains a digital signature, or other digital certificate that uses public key technology obtained through one of the above methods.

If you are going to use children's personal information only for internal purposes, that is, you will not be disclosing the information to third parties or making it publicly available, then you can use any of the above methods, or you can use what is referred to as the "e-mail plus" mechanism. The "e-mail plus" mechanism allows you to request (in the direct notice to the parent) that the parent provide consent in an e-mail message. However, this mechanism requires that you take an additional step after receiving the parent's e-mail consent to confirm that it was, in fact, the parent who provided consent (the "plus" factor). These additional steps include:

- Requesting in your initial e-mail seeking consent that the parent include a phone or fax number or mailing address in the reply e-mail, so that you can follow up to confirm consent via telephone, fax, or postal mail; or
- After a reasonable time delay, sending another e-mail to the parent to confirm consent. In this confirmatory e-mail, you should include all the original information contained in the direct notice, inform the parent that he or she can revoke the consent, and inform the parent how to revoke the consent.

You do have the option of restricting children under 13 from playing your game. However, be mindful not to design your age collection input screens in a manner that encourages children to provide a false age in order to gain access to your site. If you take reasonable measures to screen for age, then you are not responsible if a child misstates his or her age.

- Ask age information in a neutral manner at the point where you invite visitors to provide personal information or to create their log-in user ID.
- Ensure that the data entry point allows users to enter their age accurately. An example of a neutral age-screen would be a system that allows a user to freely enter month, day, and year of birth. A site that includes a drop-down menu that permits users to enter only birth years making them 13 or older, would not be considered a neutral age-screening mechanism since children cannot enter their correct age on that site.
- Do not encourage children to falsify their age information, for example, by stating that visitors under 13 cannot participate on your website or should ask their parents before participating.
- A site that does not ask for neutral date of birth information but rather simply includes a check box stating "I am over 12 years old" would not be considered a neutral age-screening mechanism.
- Use a temporary or a permanent cookie to prevent children from back-buttoning to enter a different age.

If you ask participants to enter age information, and then you fail to either screen out or obtain parental consent from those participants who indicate that they are under 13, you may be liable for violating COPPA. COPPA violations may result in steep fines from the United States Federal Trade Commission. For example, in 2008, Sony BMG settled a COPPA violation by agreeing to pay

$1 million in civil penalties, the largest COPPA settlement ever at that time.

If all this sounds onerous, that's because it is. This is the price you have to pay if you want to market to children under 13.

The above information provides only a basic introduction to COPPA. The actual text of COPPA is quite short, and is included on the attached CD. The substantive portion is located at 13 U.S.C. sec. 1303. The Federal Trade Commission (FTC) rules implementing COPPA are also included on the attached CD (current as of May 9, 2011).

In addition, the FTC website contains very helpful information regarding COPPA at:

General COPPA Guidance: http://www.ftc.gov/privacy /privacyinitiatives/childrens.html

COPPA FAQs: http://www.ftc.gov/privacy/coppafaqs.shtm.

The COPPA FAQs are extremely helpful, and while they might not answer every question, they are worth reviewing. When in doubt, err on the side of protecting the under-13 user, and a little common sense goes a long way!

TAKE NOTE! *Once you know that a user is under 13 and you have collected personal information, you have only two options: 1) You can collect their parents' e-mail addresses to provide direct notice and implement COPPA's parental consent requirements; or 2) If you do not wish to implement the COPPA protections for visitors under age 13, you may configure your data system to automatically delete the personal information of those visitors under 13 and direct them to content, if available, that does not involve collection or disclosure of personal information.*

8

PUBLISHING YOUR GAME

By Ross Dannenberg

There comes a time in the development cycle of every game where you have to pull the trigger and release your game. But under what conditions? Do you have an agreement with a publisher to publish the game? Do you sell the game on your own website? Perhaps you are a mobile game developer and you plan on selling through the Apple or Android stores. Are you developing a game for Xbox Live Arcade? The proliferation of the Internet, casual games, and stores for mobile applications have breathed new life into the video game publishing business, much to the chagrin of large, established publishers. Why? Well, chances are that if you are reading this book, you are more likely to be a small or indie developer, rather than a developer working on a game with a multimillion dollar budget and a phat publishing agreement with a major publisher (e.g., Electronic Arts, Take Two, Activision Blizzard, Ubisoft, etc.). So if you are publishing through

Apple, Android, Xbox Live Arcade, or another turnkey development channel, then there isn't much for us to discuss. But just in case you are looking to work with a publisher, there are a number of principles to keep in mind. Even if you are publishing through a turnkey development channel, knowledge of the following issues is still invaluable.

Developers often have less leverage when bargaining with a publisher. After all, the publisher is the one most likely footing the bill. So what can a developer do to ensure that it gets the best deal possible? For starters, make sure you differentiate between "best deal possible" versus "ideal contract." Stated slightly differently, prepare yourself for the very real possibility that you will not get everything you want. Decide what issues are deal-breakers for you, and what issues you are willing to negotiate to get the deal done. Be willing to compromise, but stick to your guns on those key issues. So what issues are we talking about? Here is a quick summary of the major points in any publishing agreement.

- *Grant of Rights*. Who owns the intellectual property? Under what terms? This likely depends on who came up with the idea for the game. If you, as a developer, are just coding the game based on ideas, concepts, and a game design provided by the publisher, then the publisher will likely own the IP. However, if you came up with the game concept, characters, artwork, and so on, then consider what scope of rights actually *need* to be granted or licensed to the publisher. The license grant can be based on platform (Xbox, PS, Android, etc.), geographic area, or by time. Other permutations or combinations are also possible, so consider alternatives, and be willing to get creative. Also consider who owns the right to create version 2 or any other sequel to your game.
- *Merchandising Rights*. Which came first: the video game or the movie? Nowadays, you never know. Video games have been created based on movies, and movies have been created based on video games. Ditto for books and comic books. Who owns the right to create such works? When possible, keep these rights to produce a secondary income stream if your game is popular.
- *Reserved Rights*. If a portion of your game is indispensible to you or to your ability to create additional games in the future, you should specifically call these portions out in the agreement and reserve rights to the developer for future use. For example, perhaps the developer wants to make a spin-off based on a single character in the game. Or maybe the developer wants or needs to reuse portions of the underlying code (e.g., development tools, programs, or subroutines that perform various functions not specific to one game). Just keep in mind that, even though you are reserving rights to some of the game code or technology, the publisher will still get a nonexclusive right to use the reserved material.
- *Compensation*. This is a big one. There are a few primary payment schemes, but the possibilities are endless. The most common scenario

is an advance payment made by the publisher to the developer, but that advance payment counts toward royalties earned. The advance payment is commonly nonrefundable, which means that even if the game is a flop, the developer gets to keep the advance payment. However, if the developer never completes the game in the first place, the developer will be required to refund the advance to the publisher if the advance payment was made before the release of the game. Thus, if you receive a $50,000 advance payment against royalties of $1.00 per unit sold, and the game sells only 20,000 copies, the publisher will not have to pay you any additional money. However, once the game sells more than 50,000 copies, then additional royalties will be due.

- *Gross or Net Revenue.* Even if royalties are based on units sold, royalties can be based on a percentage of gross revenue or net revenue. Royalties based on gross revenue do not take into account the publisher's overhead, such as marketing, printing, and shipping. Royalties based on net revenue, or net receipts, deduct specified costs from gross revenue, and then the royalty is based on whatever is left. Royalties based on gross revenue are easier to calculate, whereas royalties based on net revenue result in smaller royalty payments to the developer because the publisher can deduct overhead expenses "off the top." As a result, a developer will likely have to settle for a smaller royalty based on gross revenue than if the royalty were based on net revenue. However, if the royalty is based on gross revenue, then the developer doesn't have to worry about the publisher "cooking the books" to make it appear as if the game made less money than it actually did.[1] If net revenue is used, be sure to define net revenue so that shipping, taxes, promotional copies, discounts, and returns are deductible from the gross receipts, but no deduction is given for distribution fees or overhead. Deductions should be specific and limited. Avoid inclusion of broad and general deductions such as "distribution fees" and "overhead." If deductions can be limited, then a developer is likely to get a fairer share when royalties are based on net revenues.

- *Fixed Royalties.* As an alternative to a royalty per unit sold, a publisher might offer to pay a fixed royalty, e.g., $10,000 per week. There are advantages and disadvantages to such a scenario. The primary advantage to the developer is that the developer receives fixed income regardless of how well the game sells. The primary disadvantage to the developer is that, if the game is a huge success, the developer misses out on a share of the profits. The publisher thereby assumes the risk of the game selling poorly, but the publisher gets the big reward if the game is a smash hit. As a developer, if you want guaranteed income, consider requesting a substantial advance payment with a smaller ongoing royalty. You can thus

---

1. The authors have no knowledge of any actual scenario where this occurred in the video game industry. However, it is a common concern between publishers and developers, just as it is between filmmakers and distributors. Thus, a smaller royalty based on gross revenue can avoid the concern altogether.

get guaranteed money up front and have a (smaller) share in the profits if the game is a success.

- *Adjustable Royalty.* Typical royalties are in the 5 percent to 20 percent range of net receipts, and most deals end up in the 10 percent to 15 percent range. One permutation to consider is a sliding royalty scale, where the percentage increases as sales increase. This allows the publisher to recoup its overhead on initial sales, and then the developer gets a larger share of the profits once the game has reached "license to print money" status. For example, the royalty might be 10 percent for the first 20,000 units sold, and then increase to 15 percent for each additional unit sold. Different royalties might also apply to units sold through different sales channels, e.g., direct sales, mail order, foreign sales, and so on.

- *Audits/Accounting.* The developer typically has a right to audit the publisher's financial records a specified number of times during the term of the contract. It is not unusual for a developer to have the right to audit the publisher's books once per year, every other year, or up to once every third year, at the developer's discretion. Keep in mind the developer is typically required to pay for the audit. However, if the developer finds a discrepancy of more than, say, 5 percent in the royalty owed by the publisher, the clause may further subject the publisher to a financial penalty (e.g., reimburse the cost of the audit, pay interest on back owed royalties, etc.).

- *Interest.* If the publisher is not timely in making its payments according to the agreed schedule (e.g., monthly, quarterly), then late payments should be subject to an interest charge. The interest should be specified in the agreement, and typically falls within the 1 percent to 10 percent range per month.

- *Security Interest.* Developers can request a security interest against any distribution agreements entered into by the publisher, as well as against the monetary proceeds from those contracts, that the publisher makes with distributors. This may give the developer preference over unsecured creditors in the event a publisher goes bankrupt. Security interests in copyrightable works should be recorded with the United States Copyright Office at the Library of Congress in Washington, D.C. (www.copyright.gov). You cannot record such a security interest in work or a distribution contract until the work itself is registered with the Copyright Office. Use a Document Cover Sheet to record the security interest. You should also register your security interest under state law in any state where the publisher has an office. Registration is accomplished by filing under the Uniform Commercial Code, form UCC-1.

- *Warranty/Indemnification.* Publishers will typically request that the developer warrants that it has good and complete title to the property, i.e., the game, that the developer is licensing. The publisher will likely also require a warranty that the game does not infringe on anyone else's rights (e.g., rights of defamation, invasion of privacy, right of publicity, patent, trademark, and copyright) and that there are no claims or litigation pending regarding the game. Publishers prefer absolute warranties, i.e., if the developer breaks a warranty, then the developer is liable even if the developer has a decent excuse. The fact that the developer made a promise under a good faith, but mistaken belief, does not relieve the developer of liability. Thus, if the developer honestly believed that his program didn't infringe anyone's copyright because he thought a piece of source code in the program was in the public domain, and even researched the source code to try to identify an owner, and he was mistaken, he will be liable for copyright infringement and for breaching his warranty to the publisher. The publisher can then seek to require that the developer reimburse the publisher for defending a lawsuit if the publisher is sued by the owner of that piece of source code. A lesser warranty is one based "to the best of one's knowledge and belief." Under this warranty if the promisor has a good faith belief that his work does not infringe the rights of others, he will not be liable for breaching his warranty, even if the work does infringe another's work. Under such a warranty, the developer promises only that, as far as he knew, he didn't infringe another's rights. If the publisher objects to such a warranty, the developer can argue that errors and omissions (E&O) insurance is available to protect against potential liability, and the insurance carrier's assets are more substantial than the developer's. If the publisher insists on an absolute warranty, a developer should try to limit it to those matters of which the developer has firsthand knowledge.
- *Delivery Milestones.* Delivery milestones are the dates on which specified versions of the software must be delivered to the publisher, e.g., alpha release, beta release, final release. Alternative milestones might be based on storyboarding, artwork completion, game engine completion, level creation, bug fixing, etc. Regardless of when bug fixing is required to be done, the publisher will likely require the developer to continue to fix any bugs identified within a specified period of time after release of the game.
- *Trademarks/Upgrades.* Who owns the name of the game? The game name may become a valuable asset. In addition, who has the right to prepare upgrades? Who can prepare sequels? Can the publisher use a different developer? Does the developer have the right of first refusal if the publisher makes an offer to a different developer?

- *Confidentiality.* Can the parties publicly discuss the terms of the publishing agreement? What about specific portions of the agreement? Compensation, at a minimum, is typically kept confidential. Total confidentiality regarding the agreement is also common.
- *Termination.* Every agreement should have a termination clause to permit a developer to terminate the agreement if the publisher is in breach, e.g., for lack of payment. The provision may allow the developer to recover money due as well as regain rights to the program that may have been assigned or licensed to the publisher. The publisher may ask to limit the grounds for termination to a "material" breach, and will want notice and time to cure any default before the developer can terminate the agreement. "Material" breaches should be defined within the agreement.
- *Conflict Resolution.* Arbitration is typically less expensive than litigation. Publishers usually have more resources to pursue litigation than developers, so they might try to avoid arbitration under the assumption that they can "litigate the developer into bankruptcy."

The above points are just a few of the items included in publishing agreements. A comprehensive list of items is shown below, not all of which are discussed above. Some of the items are pre-agreement research that should be completed prior to entering into a publishing agreement. Be sure to consider each of these issues, and if you have any questions be sure to discuss them with an attorney who has experience dealing with video game publishing agreements.

- Parties: Developer/Publisher
- Entities: Sole Proprietorship, Partnership, or Corporation?
- Due Diligence: Is publisher reputable? Does publisher handle this type of product? What is the publisher's track record?
- Grant of Rights: Ownership of Copyright, License: Exclusive or Nonexclusive, Term, Platforms, CD-ROM, Game Cartridge, Online, Territories
  - Ancillary Rights: Merchandising, Book Publishing, Sequel Program, Right of Last Refusal
  - Reserved Rights: Right to Use Portions of Work in Other Products, Right of First Negotiation, Right of Last Refusal
- Compensation: Advance, Nonrecoupable, Against Royalties, Minimum Royalty Payments, Guarantee, Right to Terminate If Shortfall
  - Royalties: Gross vs. Net Revenue, Percentage of Net Revenues, Amounts Paid, Amounts Invoiced, Deductions Allowed (e.g., taxes, freight, discounts, returns, co-op ads), Deductions Not Allowed (e.g., distribution fee, overhead), Deductions Negotiable (cost of manufacturing)
  - Fixed Royalty: Time of Payment, Installments
  - Sliding-Scale Royalties: ___% of first _____ copies sold, ___% of next ____ copies sold, ___% thereafter.

- • Royalty on Sublicenses
  - • Interest on Late Payments
- • Conflicts of Interest: Conflicts with Other Products
- • Best-Efforts Clause
- • Most-Favored-Nation Clause
- • Minimum Advertising and Promotion Requirements
  - • Limited to Direct Out of Pocket Costs?
- • Audits and Accounting
  - • Accounting: Monthly, Quarterly, Yearly
  - • Audit Rights: Location
  - • Time Limit?
  - • Reimbursement of Audit Fees If Underpayment?
  - • Reserve for Returns: (10% to 25%)
- • Delivery Requirements:
  - • Object Code Only
  - • Date for Delivery
  - • Developer Continuing Obligation for Testing and Correction
- • Technical Support of End-Users: Publisher and/or Developer (direct to end-user or via publisher)?
- • Security Interest
- • Warranties: Absolute vs. Best of Knowledge and Belief
- • Errors & Omission Insurance: Developer Named Insured
- • Termination Clause:
  - • For Breach
  - • For Shortfall
- • Arbitration
- • Venue
- • Forum
- • Choice of Law
- • Reimbursement of Attorney Fees to Enforce Contract
- • Merger Clause

There are endless possibilities for a publishing agreement. Don't let a publisher tell you that something is "standard" without consulting an attorney or someone else who has experience dealing with publishing agreements. There is no single form document that everyone uses as a starting point. Each deal is different, and each deal encompasses a unique set of circumstances that must be dealt with based on the economic realities of the situation.

Index

A

Acceptance, of risk, 60–62
Advertising, 104–106
Age, user. *See also* Children's Online
    Privacy Protection Act (COPPA)
        privacy policies and, 122
        screens asking for, 140–141
Agreements, intellectual property
    assignments and, 83–89
        contribution, 82–83
    employment
        assistance and, 75–77
        culture in, 72–73
        external disclosure and, 78–79
        intellectual property of employees
           and, 80–81
        intellectual property protection
           and, 74–75
        internal disclosures and, 79–80
        moral rights and, 76–77
        overview of, 72
        rewards in, 75–76
        shop right doctrine and, 77
        third-party rights and, 73
        timing of, 77–78
        work for hire and, 74–75
    importance of, 64
    nondisclosure, 66–72
        choosing, 67
        confidential, 70–71
        flow in information in, 67–68
        friends and family and, 66–67
        future developments and, 71–72
        one-way, 68–69
        overview of, 66
        proprietary, 70–71
        scope of, 67–68
        two-way, 69–70
    scope of, 64
    testing, 81–82
    timing of, 64–65
Antitrust law, 94–95
Arbitrary marks, 20
Arbitration, 42, 95, 148
Assignments, 83–89
    copyrights and, 84–85
    filing of, 86–88
    licenses *vs.*, 93
    rights and, 84–85
    timing in, 85–86
    trade secrets and, 85
Attorney, patent, 16
Avoidance, of risk, 53–54

B

Bankruptcy, licensing and, 96
Beta testing, 81–82
Bonds, completion, 48–49

H

Hiring
of experts, 55
risk and, 54–55
trade secrets and, 30–31

I

Idea-expression dichotomy, 2
Identification, trademark, 24–25
Incredible Technologies (IT), 4
Indemnification, 96, 147
Independence, copyright and, 3
Insomniac Games, 21, 35, 63
Insurance
business income and extra
expense, 57
business personal property, 57
claims examples, 59–60
errors and omissions, 58, 59–60
general liability, 57
licensing disputes and, 96
limits, 56–57
risk avoidance and, 55
types of, 56
workers' compensation, 57–58
Insuring, of risk, 55–60
"Intent to use" application, 22–23
Interest, publishing and, 146–147
Investors
angel and superangel, 47
venture capital, 47–48

J

John Deere, 105

K

Konami Co., Ltd, 13

L

Lanham Act, 100
Liability
end-user licensing agreement and,
112–113
terms of use agreements and, 127–
128, 132
Licensing. See also End-user license
agreement (EULA)
advertising and, 104–106
antitrust law and, 94–95
arbitration clauses in, 95
assignments vs., 93

attorney fee clause in, 95
bankruptcy and, 96
common terms in, 97–99
contracts and, 94
copies and, 93
of copyrights, 99–100
databases, 104
dates in, 97
definition of, 92
definitions in, 97–98
disputes over, 95–96
First Amendment and, 107–108
grant of permission in, 98
indemnification clauses and, 96
injunctive relief and, 95
insurance and, 96
laws governing, 94–95
of likeness, 101–102
mediation clauses in, 95
model releases and, 102
necessity of, 93
nonassignability clauses and, 96
open-source, 106–107
parties in, 97
of patents, 103
payment and, 98–99
product placement and, 104–106
public domain works and, 93
of publicity rights, 101–102
"quality control" in, 100–101
questions for lawyer on, 92–96
recitals in, 97
specific properties in, 99–104
times in, 97
of trademarks, 100–101
of trade secrets, 102–103
types of, 93–94
Likeness, 101–102
Limited liability company (LLC), 45–46
Limits, insurance, 56–57
LLC. See Limited liability company (LLC)

M

Made-up words, 20
Mediation, 41–42, 95
Merchandising, publishing and, 144
Microsoft Corporation, 14
Model Act, 28
Models, releases for, 102
Moral rights, 76–77
MUD, 106–107

About the Contributors

» ROSS DANNENBERG (Editor; Introduction and Chapters 1, 6, 7, & 8)

Ross Dannenberg is an attorney and senior partner with the law firm of Banner & Witcoff in Washington, D.C. Ross handles a wide range of intellectual property issues, including patents, copyrights, and trademarks, working primarily with software developers. Ross has been working extensively with video game developers since 2005, when he started PatentArcade.com, the web's only blog dedicated to the cross section of video games and intellectual property law. Since that time, Ross has helped protect well-known game franchises, including *Halo*®, *Perfect Dark*®, *Flight Simulator*®, *Midtown Madness*, *Rockin' Bowl-O-Rama*®, and the world's largest free massive multiplayer online game, *RuneScape*®. He has also helped to protect a wide variety of mobile apps such as *Tweetie* (now *Twitter for iPhone*), *Textie*, and *Entranced*.

In addition to his work in the video game and mobile app arenas, Ross has also prepared and prosecuted hundreds of patent applications in a variety of other technical fields, including all varieties of software, social networking, game and computer hardware, telecommunications, Internet, and business methods, as well as other mechanical and electrical inventions. Ross also has experience enforcing and defending legal rights involving claims of patent infringement, copyright infringement, trademark infringement, digital millennium copyright act (DMCA) violations, computer fraud and abuse, and various business torts. Ross also assists clients with business and development-related issues, including licensing third-party content and music, preparation of web site terms of use, end-user license agreements, copyright and DMCA policies, as well as ensuring that game publishers are compliant with the Children's Online Privacy Protection Act (COPPA).

Ross was the founding chair of the American Bar Association's Committee on Computer Games and Virtual Worlds in the IT Division of the Intellectual Property Section, a position he held for three years, and is the 2011–2012 Vice-Chair of the IT Division. Ross is a member of the International Game Developers' Association (Steering Committee), is a founding member of the Video Game Bar Association, and is a Fellow of the American Bar Foundation. Ross is also an adjunct professor teaching copyright law at George Mason University School of Law. He earned a bachelor's degree in computer science from the Georgia Institute of Technology in 1994, and a juris doctor from The George Washington University Law School in 2000, where he was a member of *The Environmental Lawyer* legal journal.

In addition to a wide variety of articles and interviews appearing in publications such as *USA Today*, *ABC News*, *Bloomberg*, *PC Magazine*, and *Gamasutra*, Ross is also the executive editor of *Computer Games and Virtual Worlds: A New Frontier in Intellectual Property Law*, a book published by the ABA IP Section in 2010.

» CHRISSIE SCELSI (Chapter 2)

Chrissie Scelsi is the principal of Scelsi Entertainment and New Media Law, P.L., with offices in Port Charlotte and Orlando, Florida. She practices entertainment and intellectual property law, including but not limited to matters for clients in music, film, video games, and interactive and social media, as well as copyright, trademark, and general business counseling. Ms. Scelsi is also assistant legal counsel at Bohemia Interactive Simulations, a game-based simulations company in Orlando, Florida. She is a member of the American Bar Association Section of Intellectual Property Law, as well as the Forum on the Entertainment and Sports Industries. She is a Young Lawyer Fellow for the Section of Intellectual Property Law and is a member of the Annual Review Editorial Board. Ms. Scelsi is co-editor of the recent book *Computer Games and Virtual Worlds: A New Frontier in Intellectual Property Law*, published in the spring of 2010.

Ms. Scelsi graduated from Loyola University New Orleans in 2004, where she received a Bachelor of Business Administration in Marketing and also studied music business. She graduated from Saint Louis University School of Law in 2007. Ms. Scelsi can be contacted at chrissie@scelsilaw.com, or (941) 204-7363.

» SARA OWENS (Chapter 3)

Sara Owens is the leader and champion of Game Guard™, a first of its kind risk management and insurance program specifically tailored to the unique needs and risks of the video game industry. It was Sara's passion for both video games and business management that led her to create this proprietary program. Since the inception of Game Guard™, Sara has worked in conjunction with start-up developers, multi-national publishers, and everyone in-between. Sara has an unwavering commitment to the gaming industry. She understands the gaming revolution, with its explosive growth and its effect on the broader entertainment industry. Sara is a graduate of Miami University of Ohio and can be reached at Sara@gnw-eg.com or Sarafrancesowens@yahoo.com, and by telephone at (818) 912-0131.

» SHAWN GORMAN (Chapter 4)

Shawn Gorman is a partner in the Chicago office of Banner & Witcoff, Ltd. and has prepared and prosecuted patent applications in a wide variety of technology areas including video games, gambling systems, and media content distribution systems. Shawn works directly with clients to combine multiple forms of intellectual property protection. In this regard, he obtains domestic and international patent rights to protect the client's core technologies, trademark protection, and enforcement of those rights through licensing and purchasing agreements. When litigation has become necessary, Shawn has handled the various aspects of patent litigation, including being part of a trial team defending a leading manufacturer of VoIP telephony devices.

Mr. Gorman earned his juris doctor degree from the Franklin Pierce Law Center, where he was senior staff editor of the *Pierce Law Review,* contended in the Jessup International Law Moot Court, and was honored to receive the Rapee Intellectual Property Scholarship.

» BENJAMIN J. SIDERS (Chapter 5)

Benjamin J. Siders is an associate with Lewis Rice in Saint Louis, Missouri, and practices in general civil litigation with a focus on computer and technology law. Mr. Siders has assisted clients with disputes over business continuity failures, outsourcing agreements, and customized software packages. Prior to law school, Mr. Siders enjoyed a software engineering career in the telecommunications, health care, and financial sectors, working primarily with client/server, threaded, and multiprocess architectures on the Unix platform. Before the maturation of the commercial online gaming market, Mr. Siders did extensive design and development work for a number of free-to-play text-based online games.

Mr. Siders earned his JD at Washington University in St. Louis, where he served as an international student mentor, a research assistant, a senior editor on *Washington University Law Review*, and interned at the United States Attorney's office.

» C. ANDY MU (Chapter 6)

C. Andy Mu is a partner in the Washington, D.C., office of Banner & Witcoff, Ltd. He has experience in a broad range of intellectual property issues in a variety of fields including Internet technologies, business methods, telecommunications, mechanical devices, and computer software. In addition to having prepared and prosecuted numerous patent applications, Mr. Mu has experience in managing large patent portfolios; drafting freedom to operate, noninfringement, and invalidity opinions, and assisting in litigation matters and client counseling. Mr. Mu has also lectured on copyright law at the George Mason University School of Law. Mr. Mu represents a diverse spectrum of clients ranging from individuals to Fortune 500 companies.

In the gaming arena, Mr. Mu has successfully prosecuted utility and design patents relating to arcade game systems, game consoles, multi-player video game features, and video game user interfaces. Mr. Mu is also a regular contributor to the *Patent Arcade*, an online blog focused on video game patent issues.

Mr. Mu earned a BS in mechanical engineering and a BS in computer science both from the University of Maryland. He earned his JD from The George Washington University Law School, where he was a member of the Mock Trial Board.

» RAJIT KAPUR (Chapter 6)

Rajit Kapur is an associate in the Washington, D.C., office of Banner & Witcoff, Ltd. His practice encompasses multiple aspects of intellectual property law, including the procurement and enforcement of trademarks, copyrights, design patents, and utility patents in a variety of technical fields. He is also a contributor to the Banner & Witcoff *Patent Arcade* blog. Recently, Mr. Kapur has prepared and prosecuted several patent applications directed to different types of smartphone applications, including video game applications and social networking applications. Mr. Kapur received his Bachelor of Science in Mechanical Engineering, *magna cum laude*, from Tufts University in 2006 and his juris doctor from The George Washington University Law School in 2009.

» DAVE DIXON (Illustrations)

Dave Dixon is an artist with a wide and varied background in media, from traditional to digital, including not just visual arts, but music and written works as well. In addition to literary illustration, Mr. Dixon has done logo work for small businesses, mural work, and various individually commissioned pieces. Specifically in the realm of video games, Mr. Dixon has experience in concept art, character and location design, storyboarding, and menu and overlay design. A gamer and artist since the arcade heyday of the early 1980s, he is well-versed in the multimedia experience of the video game, from both sides of the screen. Mr. Dixon can be reached at ddixonva@gmail.com.